CULTURES OF THE WORLD
Kenya

Cavendish
Square
New York

Published in 2014 by Cavendish Square Publishing, LLC
303 Park Avenue South, Suite 1247, New York, NY 10010

Third Edition

This publication is published with arrangement with Marshall Cavendish International (Asia) Pte Ltd.

Copyright © 2014 Marshall Cavendish International (Asia) Pte Ltd.

Website: cavendishsq.com

Cultures of the World is a registered trademark of Times Publishing Limited.

This publication represents the opinions and views of the author based on his or her personal experience, knowledge, and research. The information in this book serves as a general guide only. The author and publisher have used their best efforts in preparing this book and disclaim liability rising directly or indirectly from the use and application of this book.

CPSIA Compliance Information: Batch #WW14CSQ

All websites were available and accurate when this book was sent to press.

Library of Congress Cataloging-in-Publication Data
Pateman, Robert.
Kenya / by Robert Pateman and Josie Elias.
 p. cm. — (Cultures of the world)
Includes index.
ISBN 978-0-76148-012-9 (hardcover) ISBN 978-1-62712-623-6 (paperback) ISBN 978-0-76148-020-4 (ebook)
1. Kenya — Juvenile literature. I. Pateman, Robert, 1954-. II. Title.
DT433.522 P38 2014
967.62 —d23

Writers: Robert Pateman and Josie Elias
Editor: Mindy Pang
Designer: Bernard Go

PICTURE CREDITS
Cover: © Cultura Travel / Philip Lee Harvey
Audrius Tomonis – www.banknotes.com: 135 • Corbis / Click Photos: 29, 94 • Getty Images: 25, 26 • Inmagine.com / Alamy: 1, 3, 5, 6, 9, 10, 13, 14, 16, 18, 19, 20, 22, 24, 30, 32, 34, 36, 38, 39, 42, 44, 45, 46, 47, 48, 50, 52, 55, 56, 59, 60, 62, 63, 65, 66, 67, 68, 70, 72, 75, 76, 77, 79, 82, 88, 89, 90, 91, 95, 98, 100, 101, 103, 104, 106, 107, 108, 110, 111, 113, 116, 117, 119, 120, 122, 123, 124, 125, 126, 127, 128, 129, 130, 131

PRECEDING PAGE
An aerial view of the Nabuyatom Crater south of Lake Turkana in Kenya.

Printed in the United States of America

CONTENTS

KENYA TODAY

KENYA GAINED INDEPENDENCE FROM BRITAIN ON DECEMBER 12, 1963. Although the young country was made up of people from many different ethnic groups, the concept of a modern Kenyan nation was enthusiastically accepted. For many years this East African country was considered one of the continent's success stories. Kenyan farms cultivated coffee and tea for export, while the factories produced many goods that Kenyans needed. The game parks and beaches attracted tourists from all over the world.

The presidential election of 2007 was won by Mwai Kibaki but the opposition candidate Raila Odinga rejected the result and the European Union Election Observer Mission noted that the presidential elections lacked credibility and did not meet international standards.

Rival ethnic groups met Kibaki's reelection with communal violence. Government security forces reacted to the unrest and over 1,100 people were killed and a further 600,000 people were displaced. The African Union asked Kofi Annan to help negotiate a power-sharing deal between Odinga and Kibaki. After an agreement was reached in 2008 a Grand Coalition Government with Raila Odinga as prime minister was sworn-in.

A class of secondary school students having their lessons at Sagam Village. The government introduced plans to offer free secondary education in 2008.

The Kofi Annan mediation process recommended that reforms be undertaken to prevent future contentious elections. These reforms include a complete overhaul of the elections process and the establishment of a new independent elections commission. It was advised that there also be judicial and police reform. A new constitution providing for these and other reforms was approved in 2010.

Kenya's case was referred to the International Criminal Court (ICC) in 2009 to try the perpetrators of the postelection violence. In 2012 ICC judges confirmed charges against four Kenyans, including Deputy Prime Minister Uhuru Kenyatta, a former Education Minister, the former head of Public Service, and a radio presenter. They are now awaiting trial at the ICC over their alleged role in Kenya's postelection violence in 2008.

The political instability and corruption in Kenya have caused great problems for the country. Foreign aid and loans have been withdrawn or delayed because of corruption. In 2003 Kenya announced a program to introduce free schools for all children. Over 1 million children who had never attended school before were enrolled in the education system. Free Primary Education (FPE) brought some positive changes but was still out of reach of many Kenyan families. The government increased funding to the education sector but many international donors were assisting the government with financial aid. Following the UK's decision to stop contributing to Kenya's aid program in 2009, the United States announced that they were going to stop giving to Kenya's education programs in 2010. It had been discovered that more than $1 million was missing and $26 million had been diverted from the education fund. The UK's funding totaled $88.8 million over a 5-year period, beginning in 2005. The last tranche of funding that amounted to $16.1 million was withheld.

There are problems with FPE in Kenya. Rapid expansion of the schools has led to an increased number of teacher to student ratio and an overall lowering of the standard of education. More children are able to take the Certificate of Primary Education exam, but the percentage of passes has decreased. Even so, the FPE initiative is commendable. Combatting corruption has to be a priority to ensure that the allocated funds from both the Kenyan government and foreign aid packages go toward FPE.

It has been estimated that over 50 percent of the population in Kenya lives below the poverty line. Approximately 60 percent of Nairobi's population, that is 2.5 million people, lives in about 200 settlements in Nairobi, occupying just 6 percent of the land. In the people's settlements many families send their children to informal schools funded by Non-Governmental Organizations (NGOs). Children who cannot afford to buy a uniform and school meals or pay for transportation to a public school can go to an informal school and, at least, have the opportunity of an education. Most of the informal schools do not have electricity, running water, or toilets.

Kibera is the biggest slum in Africa, and one of the biggest in the world. The average shack can be home to eight people or more, and it is 12 feet by 12 feet, built with mud walls and with a dirt or concrete floor. Only 20 percent of Kibera has electricity. The aid group UN-Habitat is in the process of providing electricity to some parts of Kibera but most people cannot afford to pay the connection fee. Until recently residents of Kibera had to collect their water from the Nairobi Dam. The water is not clean and can be the cause of cholera and typhoid outbreaks. Now there are two mains water pipes into Kibera, one from the municipal council and the other sponsored by the World Bank. UN-Habitat is trying to improve sanitation facilities in Kibera. One latrine is shared by up to 50 shacks and there are hardly any toilets. The latrines are emptied by young boys who carry the contents to the river. This increases the risk of waterborne diseases. Kibera is near the industrial area of Nairobi where up to 50 percent of the available workforce is employed. The majority of the rest of the workforce is unemployed. That is why education, training, and teaching of skills are vital.

There has been a high level of urban migration in Kenya, as people from the countryside move to the cities in search of work. The pastoralist community of northern Kenya has had to contend with severe droughts and severe flooding in recent years. Four of the 28 major droughts of the past 100 years occurred in the last 10 years, resulting in a devastating impact on people's lives and livelihoods. It has been estimated that 1 million people in northern Kenya are now living in new villages where they are almost entirely dependent on food aid, or they have migrated to the cities in search of work.

Clashes over water and pasture have significantly increased with the drought. Water scarcity has forced people to migrate. Food insecurity has resulted in population displacement and deaths from fighting over available water points and pasture. Drought and famine-related stress has led to increased cattle-rustling and banditry, and the clashes have intensified as Kenya struggles with a food crisis estimated to be affecting approximately 10 million people.

The world's biggest refugee camp is Dadaab in eastern Kenya. It was originally built to house 90,000 refugees but is currently home to more than 500,000 refugees, mostly from neighboring Somalia. Some of the refugees arrived in the camp more than 20 years ago. The management of the camp was taken over by the United Nations Refugee Agency (UNHCR) in the early 1990s. Refugees arrive on a daily basis and it is becoming increasingly difficult to guarantee health and dignity to the residents. The international community and aid agencies have been asked to give greater assistance to the Kenyan government in hosting the refugees, but this will not be a long-term solution. In spite of a meeting by key stakeholders in June 2012 to discuss the future of Dadaab refugee camp there has been no consensus on a way forward.

Election-related violence and the displacement of people as a result of clashes or natural disasters have affected thousands of families in Kenya for many years. In April 2012 a landslide in the Mathare slum area of Nairobi killed six people and destroyed at least 40 homes. In 2008 electoral violence left approximately 500,000 people displaced and of these there were still approximately 1,500 people in temporary camps in 2012. These camps are often without health facilities or adequate security. A bill tabled in parliament in June 2012 requires that the government protect internally displaced persons (IDPs). The bill calls for the establishment of a fund to assist the IDPs and includes the clause that heavy fines be imposed on anyone who blocks the resettlement of IDPs, embezzles funds, or steals supplies.

Nairobi has a reputation for being a dangerous city and has struggled with a rising crime rate for many years. Crime has risen as a result of unplanned urbanization and poor security infrastructure. Most wealthy Kenyans live in Nairobi, a cosmopolitan and multicultural city with a strong British presence. Many residents of Nairobi enjoy a wealthy lifestyle and take pleasure in the bustling city center, going to the restaurants, bars, coffeehouses, movie theaters, and shopping malls. The city is the center of the Kenyan music scene. *Benga* is a Kenyan genre developed in Nairobi and is a fusion of jazz and Luo music. Nairobi National Park is close to the city center and it is a popular place to visit to escape the traffic and noise of city life. Elephants, giraffe, and zebra roam in the park, silhouetted against the city skyline. There are many parks and open spaces throughout Nairobi.

Nairobi downtown and central business district has many skyscrapers that are the headquarters of local and international businesses and corporations. Various commercial buildings are being constructed to accommodate the demand for office floorspace in the city. Traffic congestion is a problem in Nairobi but Africa's ubiquitous minibuses, called *matatus* in Kenya, are widely available and are the most popular form of transportation. *Matutas* are distinguishable by their colorful decoration and are usually equipped with loud sound systems and television screen in a bid to attract more customers.

There have been recent bomb attacks in Nairobi. In March 2012 hand grenades were thrown at a bus station and at a bar, killing nine people. In May 2012 an explosion in a shopping mall injured 28 people. On September 21, 2013, terrorists attacked the Westgate shopping mall in Nairobi resulting in the deaths of 72 people. These acts of violence have led to heightened security in the city.

Kenya is world famous for its safari parks. Within the country there are more than 40 national parks and reserves that have been set aside for the conservation of national habitat and wildlife. The Masai Mara National Reserve is home to many Masai pastoralists and is also famous for the annual wildebeest migration when thousands of animals migrate across the plains in search of grass after the rains.

Kenya is a land of contrasts. It boasts unspoilt tropical beaches to snow-covered mountains, open savannah plains to gentle rolling hills. There are nomads in the arid regions, mud huts in isolated rural communities, and modern high rise housing in the cities. However, through 50 years of independence, a rapidly growing population and severe droughts has put great pressure on the country's natural resources. Widespread corruption hampers economic development and makes life difficult for Kenyans. As president of Kenya, Uhuru Kenyatta of The National Alliance (TNA) party faces great challenges in his efforts to steer Kenya to a brighter future.

The skyline of Nairobi. Despite the different problems that plague the capital, it is still an established hub for business and culture. The Nairobi Stock Exchange, for example, is one of the largest in Africa.

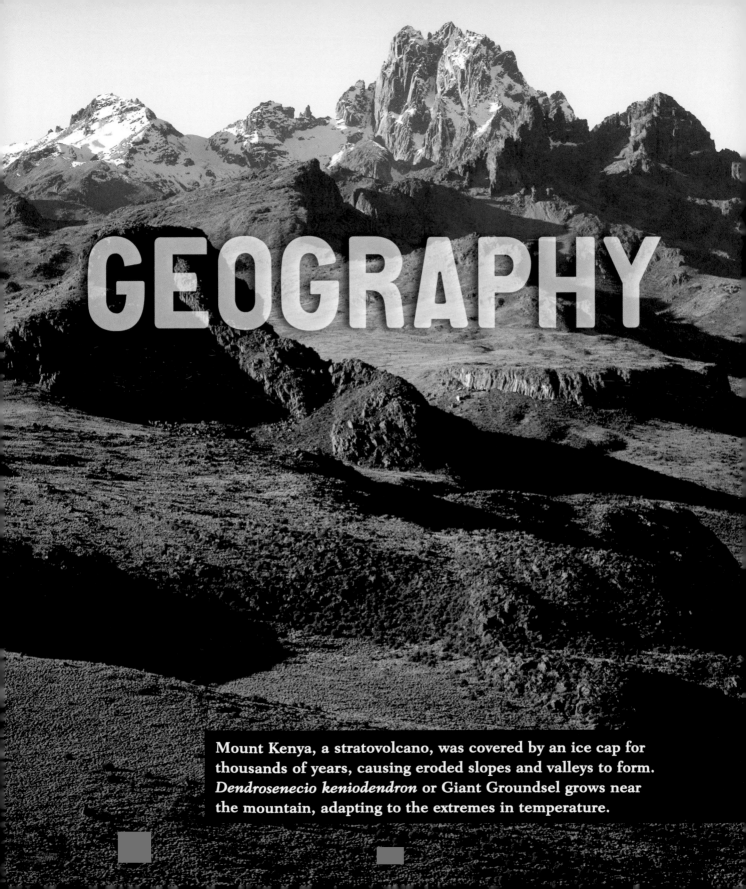

GEOGRAPHY

Mount Kenya, a stratovolcano, was covered by an ice cap for thousands of years, causing eroded slopes and valleys to form. *Dendrosenecio keniodendron* or Giant Groundsel grows near the mountain, adapting to the extremes in temperature.

1

KENYA IS SITUATED ON the eastern coast of Africa. It shares borders with five countries: Tanzania to the south, Uganda to the west, South Sudan and Ethiopia to the north, and Somalia to the east. It also has an eastern coastline that is bounded by the Indian Ocean. The equator runs through the center of the country.

Covering 224,961 square miles (582,646 square km), Kenya is about the same size as Texas. It is divided into five main geographical regions: the Lake Victoria basin, the northern semiarid desert, the eastern plateau forelands, the Rift Valley and other highlands, and the coastal areas.

Much of northern Kenya is semiarid desert, so 85 percent of the population is crowded into the fertile and wettest, southern two-thirds of the country. In recent years more and more people have moved to the cities to try to find work. The vast majority of Kenya's population are subsistence farmers, who depend on a small plot of land for their survival.

CLIMATE AND SEASONS

Kenya has a tropical climate on the coast and an arid interior. The twice-yearly changes in the weather pattern are marked by rainfall. Rainfall in Kenya is bimodal, which means that the country has two rainy seasons. In a typical year, the long rains arrive in April and last until June. The short rains generally start in October and may last until December. But this pattern can vary in different regions.

The geography of Kenya is varied and diverse. The country stretches from the Indian Ocean in the east up to the snow-capped mountains in the north. The terrain changes from low-lying coastal plains up to the Kenyan highlands with Batian, the tallest peak of Mount Kenya, reaching 17,058 feet (5,197 m).

Various national parks are found in the Great Rift Valley, which attract countless outdoor adventure enthusiasts.

The short rains usually fall more in the mornings, followed by long periods of afternoon sunshine. The long rains bring heavier, more regular, and long-lasting rainstorms. The two rainy seasons last for approximately three months each, but far more rain falls during the long rains.

January and February, and then August through September, are very dry months when many rivers and lakes dry up completely. In recent years Kenya has suffered from extreme weather conditions, with regional droughts being followed by heavy floods. In Mombassa, Malindi, and the coastal regions it is humid and hot with about 41 inches (104.1 cm) of rain a year. Areas of high altitude such as the Lake Victoria Basin and the highland regions to the north and south of Kisumu have an average annual rainfall of 75 inches (190 cm) and a mean annual temperature of 80°F (26.6°C).

The low plateau area north of the equator is extremely dry. For a short period in April the region receives rain, but the rains are unpredictable. For much of the year, the rivers are only dry, sandy beds.

Temperatures in Kenya vary more with altitude than with the time of year. The temperatures average 80°F (26.6°C) along the coast, which has an elevation of between sea level and 1,312 feet (400 m). In contrast, Nairobi lies at an altitude of 5,500 feet (1,680 m) and has far lower temperatures. Indeed, evenings in the capital can be down to 55°F (12.7°C).

THE GREAT RIFT VALLEY

The Great Rift Valley is a fissure 4,000 miles (6,437 km) long in the earth's crust. The valley starts in Jordan and stretches to Mozambique. In East Africa it breaks into two branches, one of which passes through Kenya. The course of the valley becomes quite clear if seen from the outer space, because it is marked by a series of lakes. On the ground it is not always so obvious. At Lake Turkana in northern Kenya, it is almost impossible to tell that one is standing in a valley. Farther south, cliffs of 2,000 to 3,000 feet (610 to 914 m) tall rise dramatically from the valley floor.

MOUNTAINS

Much of Kenya is mountainous. Within the Kenyan Highlands are two major mountain ranges running north to south on either side of the Great Rift Valley. To the west lies the Mau Escarpment and to the east the Aberdare Range. Mount Kenya is located east of the highlands. At 17,058 feet (5,197 m) it is the highest mountain in the country and the second highest in Africa, after Mount Kilimanjaro in Tanzania. There are several glaciers on the slopes, and the top is covered with snow throughout the year. The mountain sits virtually on the equator and forms a dramatic border between Kenya's highlands and lowlands. The higher slopes of Mount Kenya receive heavy rainfall. The rain that flows down the slopes makes the area below some of the most fertile farmland in the country. Kenya's second highest mountain is Mount Elgon. It is located much farther west on the Kenyan-Ugandan border. At 14,178 feet (4,320 m), it is high enough to sometimes have snow on the summit.

Kenya's mountain slopes are the home of important rainforests that protect many rare trees, plants, and animals. These mountain forests also act as water catchment areas, soaking up the heavy rain and releasing the water slowly into streams and rivers. They are therefore vital in protecting the water supply for thousands of Kenyans who live and farm in the surrounding areas. Yet, less than 2 percent of Kenya is covered by forest, and even these areas are threatened by illegal logging.

NAIROBI

Nairobi is the capital of Kenya and is located in the south-central part of the country. The country's parliament is located in Nairobi. The city is also Kenya's commercial and industrial center. It is the headquarters of important regional railways, harbors, and airline corporations.

The equator runs through Kenya, and the area to the north is extremely dry. In contrast, Mount Kenya is capped with snow year-round and has several glaciers on its slopes.

Constructed in 1974, the Kenyatta International Conference Center in the central business district was the tallest building in Nairobi for more than 20 years, when it was taken over by The New Central Bank Tower in 2000.

The city is built on a plateau that is about a mile (1.6 km) above sea level, so it has a cool climate although it is close to the equator. The city is considered to be free of malaria, unlike other East African cities where malaria is a public health problem.

Nairobi was founded in 1899 when the railroad that was being built from the coast reached the area. The area was known as Enkare Nairobi, or the place of cool waters, by the few Masai who grazed their cattle in the region. As the last flat ground before the steep Great Rift Valley escarpment, the British chose Nairobi as the site for a base camp. Almost overnight, an enormous tent camp grew up to house thousands of railroad workers. A permanent settlement was never planned here. Nevertheless, Nairobi became the natural town to serve the needs of the white farmers who slowly settled along the railroad line. During the colonial period, Nairobi became the most important town in British East Africa. Today, the railroad provides the largest number of jobs in the industrial sector in Nairobi.

Nairobi has many modern facilities, including an international airport, sports stadiums, and three universities. The Kenyatta International Conference Center is the city's most famous landmark. Many important trade fairs and conferences are staged in Nairobi, and there are international standard sports facilities, such as Nyayo National Stadium. Nairobi is also famous for the Nairobi National Park, where it is possible to photograph wildlife with the city skyline in the background.

In recent years Nairobi's reputation for being a modern and beautiful city has been overshadowed by serious social problems caused by a rapidly growing population. The population has grown over the years from 11,500 inhabitants in 1906 to over 3.1 million in 2012. In 2009 it was estimated that more than half of the city's population live in overcrowded informal settlements and slums that occupy less than 5 percent of Nairobi's residential area. The majority of the new arrivals are poor farmers from the countryside who usually end up living in one of the slum areas, such as Kibera or the Mathare Valley.

Poverty has contributed to a rising crime rate, and Nairobi is sometimes referred to as "Nairobbery." Few people choose to walk around the city center after dark, while people living in the upper-class suburbs often lock themselves in their houses at night and employ security guards.

MOMBASA

With a population of approximately 940,000 people Mombasa is about one-third the size of Nairobi. It is built on an island in a bay of the Indian Ocean and has a much longer history than the capital. The first Arab traders founded Mombasa in the 11th century. The old part of the city consists of narrow winding streets and Arab-style houses. For a short time at the end of the 16th century, the city was controlled by the Portuguese, who built Fort Jesus to guard the entrance to the old harbor. The fort is well preserved and is one of Kenya's most important historic buildings. Mombasa has two ports: Mombasa Old Port on the east side of the island and Kilindini Harbor on the west side of the island. Kilindini dominates the commercial life of the city and has enabled it to become the site of Kenya's oil refining industry. Many factories have also been built to take advantage of the harbor facilities. Industries include metal and cement works, shipbuilding and repair, a fertilizer plant, and sugar processing. Work has been undertaken to improve the port facilities. The Mombasa Port Development project includes the construction of a new cargo berth and dredging in the Kilindini channel. This will enable bigger container ships to come into the harbor and allow two-way traffic through the channel.

OTHER CITIES

Nakuru is the most important town in the Kenyan Highlands. It has a population of approximately 1.6 million people and is an important agricultural center. Kisumu is the capital of Nyanza Province on the northeastern shore of Lake Victoria. The town is the commercial and industrial hub for the western part of the country and has good transportation links to Mombasa. Eldoret is in the fertile area of the highlands. It is an important farming region and its main crops are corn, wheat, and pyrethrum. It is the seat of a Roman Catholic bishopric and is home to the University of Moi. Lamu is a port, town, and island in the Indian Ocean. It has a population of approximately 100,000 people. Lamu Old Town is the best preserved Swahili settlement in East Africa and has continuously been inhabited for over 700 years. It was added to the United Nations Educational, Scientific and Cultural Organization (UNESCO) World Heritage list in 2001.

FLORA

This flowering plant, also known as *adenium obesum*, commonly grows in the country. It is used for medicinal purposes despite being known as poisonous.

Since Kenya has so many different regions, it is home to a marvellous range of flowers, shrubs, and trees. After the rains, even the desert blooms. A good example of the variety of Kenyan plant life is seen on the slopes of Mount Elgon, where the forest contains 62 different species of trees. In contrast, it would be very unusual to find a forest in North America or Europe that had more than 25 different species. Some trees such as Elgon teak (*Olea capensis*) dominate the forest. Sadly, many of Kenya's native trees, such as the baobab (*Adansonia digitata*), take a long time to grow. If they are cut for commercial purposes, they are often replaced with fast-growing species from Australia or South America.

Each region in Kenya has unique flora. Along the coast, palms and mangroves are the most typical plants. The dry plains and northern areas are dominated by low bush, scrub, and grassland. The highlands were originally covered in forest, much of which has now been cleared. African camphor (*Ocotea usambarensis*), African olive (*Olea europaea ssp. africana*), and the African pencil cedar (*Juniperus procera*) are typical trees of this region. The African pencil tree gets its name from years of use in the manufacture of pencils. It is the only juniper found in sub-Saharan Africa where the old forest groves of this species are being depleted by logging. The larger trees are prized for timber used in fence posts, roof shingles, furniture, cabinet making, and pencils.

The baobab is probably Kenya's most famous tree. It is found in many different parts of the country and can grow in the drier areas if there is underground water. It has a strange upside-down appearance that makes it seem as though its roots are sticking into the air and its trunk into the ground. Its trunk can be hollowed out to make canoes or water holders; the bark is fire resistant and can be made into cloth; the bark fibers can be twisted into ropes and baskets; the leaves and fruit pulp are made into medicine; and the seeds and leaves are edible. The fruit, called monkey bread, is rich in vitamin C. Radio-carbon dating has dated some baobab trees at over 2,000 years old.

FAUNA

Kenya is famous for its abundant and varied wildlife. The country has developed an extensive network of national parks, reserves, and sanctuaries to help protect its precious natural heritage.

Insects and arachnids are by far the most numerous and diverse in Kenya's animal kingdom. There are approximately 1,000 species of butterflies alone. Perhaps the most dramatic of the insects are the termites, some species of which build great towering nests above the plains. Their nests are made from earth, cemented together with the termites' droppings and saliva until they are as hard as bricks.

Lizards, birds, and frogs feed on insects, and these in turn become food for small carnivores such as mongooses, birds of prey, and snakes. There are approximately 127 species of snakes in Kenya. Of these only 18 have caused human fatalities, 6 could cause a human fatality, another 10 could cause a lot of pain, and the remaining 93 are neither nonvenemous nor dangerous.

The largest reptile in Kenya is the Nile crocodile (*Crocodylus niloticus*) that usually grows to about 20 feet (6 m) in length and is hunted and poached for its skin. Lizards range from giant monitor lizards that can grow to 6 feet (1.8 m) in length to the tiny geckos found in most homes. The unusual structure of the pads on the geckos' toes allows them to run up walls or walk across the ceiling. The larger mammals include elephants, giraffes, zebras, rhinoceroses, and antelopes.

Many animals in Kenya can live together in the same area because they have different eating habits and food preferences. Zebras, for example, nibble on grass blades, while gazelles prefer shoots that grow close to the ground. Some of the larger antelopes tend to be browsers and find their food on small trees and bushes. Elephants and giraffes graze in the tallest trees where no other animal can reach. Predators such as lions, cheetahs, and wild dogs hunt and kill for food. They tend to take the slowest and weakest animals. After the predators have made their kill, scavengers swoop in to claim their share. Vultures are often the first to arrive, quickly followed by jackals. In addition, some animals form mixed herds to benefit from each other's characteristics. Antelopes, for example, move in herds with zebras because the latter are alert to predators.

Kenya's wildlife varies from region to region. In the dry areas of the north, the reticulated giraffe (*Giraffa camelopardalis reticulata*) and Grevy's

A herd of African elephants at the Amboseli National Park. The park is the best place in Africa to get close to the free-ranging mammals.

zebra have quite different markings from the other species of giraffes and zebras elsewhere in the country. The mountain bongo antelope (*Tragelaphus eurycerus isaaci*), the giant forest hog (*Hylochoerus meinertzhageni*), and the Angolan black and white colobus monkey (*Colobus anolensis ssp palliatus*) are found in the mountainous areas.

GAME PARKS

Kenya has established an extensive network of game parks and reserves to protect its wildlife. Some of the most important parks are mentioned in the following paragraphs.

ABERDARE NATIONAL PARK Aberdare is a forest area that is home to elephants, rhinoceroses, and rare animals, such as the bongo that cannot be seen anywhere else. It covers an area of 296 square miles (767 square km) and is located in the higher areas of the Aberdare mountain ranges of Central Kenya.

AMBOSELI NATIONAL PARK Amboseli is located in the Loitoktok district of the Rift Vally Province. It offers close-up views of Mount Kilimanjaro, although the mountain is actually across the border in Tanzania. The mountain is the highest in Africa, and its peak reaches a height of 19,340 feet (5,895 m). The park is home to large herds of elephants. There have been conflicts in Amboseli with the Masai, while a large number of tourist vans have caused considerable damage to the environment.

LAKE NAKURU NATIONAL PARK Lake Nakuru is in the Nakuru district of the Rift Valley Province. It is famous for the flamingoes that migrate from other lakes in the Great Rift Valley. Being a small park it is easier to protect, so some rhinoceroses have been relocated here.

The Red List of the International Union for Conservation of Nature and Natural Resources (IUCN) names plants and animals around the world that are considered threatened. There are nine categories: extinct, extinct in the wild, critically endangered, endangered, vulnerable, near threatened, least concern, data deficient, and not evaluated.

Kenyan animals in the vulnerable category include the dugong (Dugong dugon). The dugong is one of the world's most threatened marine mammals and its population has declined by 30 percent in the past 60 years. The cheetah (Acinonyx jubatus), the African lion (Panthera leo), the African elephant (Loxodonta africana), and the crevice tortoise (Malacochersus tornieri) are also listed as vulnerable. Among endangered species in Kenya are Grevy's zebra (Equus grevyi) and the African wild dog (Lycaon pictus), while the black rhinoceros (Diceros bicornis), the hawksbill turtle (Eretmochelys imbricata), and Hunter's antelope (Beatragus hunteri) are critically endangered. The eastern red colobus monkey (Procolobus rufomitratus) was listed as critically endangered in 2000 but, thanks to conservation efforts, was reclassified to be on the list of least concern in 2008. The black rhinoceros' range has shrunk substantially due to poaching for its horn. One relatively successful approach in attempts to discourage rhinoceros poaching is dehorning, which does not affect the rhinoceros' ability to defend itself but makes it less attractive to poachers. However, black rhinoceros numbers are very low, and their chances of survival remain fragile. Hunter's antelope, also known as Hunter's hartebeest,

has been on the critically endangered list since 1996 and barely survives in northeastern Kenya near the border with Somalia. Since the 1970s, Hunter's antelope numbers have declined from 14,000 to a few hundred due to habitat destruction and poaching. Its population has declined by 90 percent since 1980.

The species in the "extinct" category is the Kenya rocky river frog (right). It is believed to have lived in rocky rivers and streams, as its name reveals, on the eastern slopes of Mount Elgon.

MASAI MARA NATIONAL RESERVE The Masai Mara lies in the Great Rift Valley and is perhaps Kenya's most famous park. It borders the Serengeti Plain in Tanzania. Huge herds of wildebeest, sometimes numbering around a million animals, migrate between the two parks and reach Kenya in July and August.

MARINE PARKS Kenya has five marine parks along its coast: Malindi, Watamu, Mombasa, Kiunga, and Kisite. The parks have beautiful coral reefs that are home to a diverse range of marine life. These parks also protect mangrove swamps that are home to birds and coconut crabs (*Cardisoma carnifex*).

MERU NATIONAL PARK Meru is an area of thorny bush land located northeast of Mount Kenya. The park has rare animals including the reticulated giraffe, Kenya gerenuk (*Litocranius walleri*), and Somali ostrich (*Struthio camelus molybdophanes*).

MOUNT ELGON NATIONAL PARK Mount Elgon is the second-tallest mountain in the country. Its slopes have many native trees and plants and large caves. Elephants and other animals enter the caves at night to find salt licks.

MOUNT KENYA NATIONAL PARK Mount Kenya is the tallest mountain in the country. The mountain and park became a biosphere reserve in 1978 and were declared a World Heritage Site by the UNESCO in 1997.

NAIROBI NATIONAL PARK Being just a half-hour drive from Nairobi city center, lions, gazelles, and antelopes are among the park's inhabitants. Some of the animals stay in the park throughout the year, while others migrate there in the dry season.

SIBILOI NATIONAL PARK Situated on the eastern side of Lake Turkana in northern Kenya, Sibiloi is an important refuge for the world's largest population of crocodiles. Other animals include lions, cheetahs, gerenuks, Grevy's zebras, and oryx. Within the park are the remains of a petrified forest that is estimated to be about 7 million years old. The petrified forest is proof that the arid park was once a dense forest that fossilized and turned into stone over a long period of time. Lake Turkana was added to the UNESCO World Heritage List in 1997.

TSAVO NATIONAL PARK Tsavo is the largest national park in Kenya and lies between Nairobi and the coast. It is divided into Tsavo East and Tsavo West. The combined area covers a total of 4 percent of Kenya's land area and makes it one of the largest national parks in the world. Some of Africa's largest herds of elephants live there, but the park is also one of the first to suffer whenever the poachers return.

OTHER PARKS Samburu, Buffalo Springs, and Shaba are in the dry north of Kenya and have many rare species of animals. However, few tourists visit them as they can be very remote.

INTERNET LINKS

www.kenyaforests.org

Official website of the Kenya Forest Working Group, who work together to promote sound forest management and conservation practices in Kenya.

www.kws.org/parks/parks_reserves/NANP.html

Official website of the Kenya Wildlife Service, with information on conservation, research projects, parks, and reserves.

www.unesco.org/new/en/

Official UNESCO website with a section on culture and detailed information on Lamu Old Town.

HISTORY

Uncovered in the 1920s, the Ruins of Gedi was once a bustling Swahili town in the 13th century. The town was comprised of a palace, a mosque for the Muslim community, and an extensive collection of complex houses furnished with bathrooms, drainage, and flush toilets.

2

KENYA AS A NATION is a modern concept. Its borders were created by the Europeans, and the early history of the land can only be told as part of the history of East Africa. The early Africans left no written record of their history, but we can learn something about them from archaeological digs as well as by studying the language, culture, and folklore of present-day African peoples.

Nevertheless, there are considerable gaps in our knowledge of Kenya's early history. Very little is known about the interior of the country before the 19th century, and our limited knowledge is based on legends shrouding early Kenyan history in mystery and myth.

BIRTHPLACE OF HUMANITY

The oldest fossil records of human existence have come from archaeological digs in Tanzania, Ethiopia, and Lake Turkana in Kenya. Some of Kenya's most important archaeological artifacts were found by Louis Leakey and his family.

Louis Leakey (1903—72), born to British missionary parents in Kenya, was an archaeologist and anthropologist. In the early 1960s, Louis and his wife, Mary (1913—96), discovered fragments of teeth and a jawbone that they estimated to belong to a 14-million-year-old ancestor of humankind. This was the earliest evidence of human evolution ever discovered.

Around 2000 B.C. the Cushite people of northern Africa moved into present-day Kenya. The Bantu arrived in about A.D. 200 and settled on the coast and later the Nilote people arrived and occupied the plains of the Great Rift Valley. Arab traders arrived in about A.D. 700 and their intermarriages with the Bantu created the beginning of the Swahili language and culture that exists in Kenya today.

Richard Leakey in 1977 with two crucial skull discoveries, the *Australopithecus* in his right hand, and the *Homo habilis* in his left hand.

Their son Richard was born in 1944 and continued their work. He found complete human skulls that were more than 2 million years old. The discoveries made by the Leakey family strongly suggest that East Africa was the birthplace of humanity. We know, on the basis of tools and cave drawings discovered there, that people using stone tools were living in the Great Rift Valley around 40,000 years ago.

However, the next part of African history remains unknown. There is little information on the hunter-gatherers who eventually came to settle in the region, although it is thought that they might be similar to the Khoisan people of southern Africa. The Khoisan people traditionally depended on hunting, gathering, and herding.

INVASION

About 2,000 years ago East Africa started to receive a massive influx of people from the west. Although many different peoples, the new arrivals spoke similar languages belonging to the Bantu group of languages. The migrants were farmers and had more advanced tools and weapons than the hunter-gatherers living in the region. These tools helped the Bantu peoples to clear forests and grow crops on the land.

The migration could have been caused by a number of factors in their place of origin, such as an increasing population that led to overcrowding, an unfavorable change in climate, or diminishing resources. One can only guess the true reasons for the migration as very little is known about the event. Yet it drastically changed the face of Africa and is one of the biggest migrations in human history.

During this time other migrations were also taking place. Nilotes and Cushities started to move in from the north and northeast. The Nilote groups included the Masai and the Samburu, who still maintain many of the ways of their migratory ancestors. It was due to these migrations that Kenya today is a nation of so many different peoples and cultures.

OUTSIDERS ARRIVE

Between the seventh and tenth centuries, Arab traders settled on the Kenyan coast. Often fleeing wars in their homeland, the Arabs built forts and cities and established trade with the interior of the country. Despite continually fighting among themselves, the Arab communities grew rich and powerful.

During the 15th century there were technological advances in shipbuilding and navigation in Europe. This allowed the Portuguese to sail around the southern tip of Africa and explore the eastern coastline. They were amazed to find wealthy Arab settlements where they had expected wilderness. The Portuguese soon established their own trading centers and for the next two centuries fought with the Arabs for control of the East African coastline. The most lasting reminder of Portuguese influence in Kenya is Fort Jesus in Mombasa. The fort, inscribed on the UNESCO World Heritage List in 2011, was built in 1593 to 1596. After many sieges it was captured by the Arabs in 1698, bringing Portuguese influence in the region to an end.

As Portugal's fortunes declined, other European powers such as Great Britain, France, and Germany began to take an interest in East Africa. European missionaries, often assisted by Arab rulers on the coast, explored the interior of the continent. In 1848 the missionary Johannes Rebmann became the first European to see Mount Kilimanjaro. The following year, 1849, Johann Krapf was the first European to see Mount Kenya. In 1858 John Speke (1827—64) became the first European to reach Lake Victoria, where he discovered what he believed to be the source of the Nile.

DIVIDING UP AFRICA

Although trade, missionary work, and exploration took place, the European powers had little political control over Africa until the 1880s. In the Berlin Conference of 1884 to 1885 it was decided which areas of Africa each

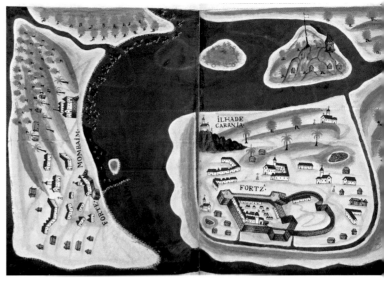

A 1646 Portuguese exploration map of Mombasa by Pedro Barretto de Resende.

Apart from Great Britain, France, Germany, Portugal, Spain, Italy, and Belgium were the other European countries that took part in what came to be known as the Scramble for Africa. The rush to colonize as many parts of Africa as possible lasted from 1876 to 1914.

THE GREAT SIEGE

The Portuguese never had a large army in Africa, and most of their supplies had to be brought in by ship from their colonies in India. The great Mombasa fortress (below), or Fort Jesus, suffered many sieges, including one from the Wasimba—fierce African warriors who became unlikely allies of the Arabs. The final and greatest siege started in March 1696, when the fortress and town were bombarded by Omani Arabs. There were only 50 Portuguese in the fort with several hundred local people.

From the beginning, food was short and the defenders had to make daring raids at night to bring in supplies. On Christmas Day, four Portuguese ships sailed into the bay and fortress, and the tiny garrison thought that they were saved. However, the fleet came under attack and had to flee, leaving the desperate defenders to their fate. Next, bubonic plague broke out, sparing only a handful of people. The Arabs did not attempt to storm the walls, and in September a fleet was able to bring in a large force of Portuguese and Indian troops to relieve the defenders.

Still the siege continued until, two years and nine months after it started, Arab soldiers finally scaled the walls. They found only a dozen survivors, whom they immediately executed. One story tells how a young boy promised to show the attackers a store of gold, only to lead them into the gunpowder storeroom, which he then blew up, killing himself and all those around him. The fort still stands today and is a popular stop for tourists. It was declared a World Heritage site by UNESCO in 2011.

European nation would have the first claim. The purpose of the conference was to prevent arguments and possible armed conflict among the European powers. The result was a scramble, as each nation raced to colonize its part of the continent.

It was agreed in Berlin that all the lands north of the middle of Lake Victoria, including Kenya and Uganda, would come under British control. This area was of particular concern to the British because they had a considerable investment in Egypt and consequently were anxious to control the source of the Nile River.

The Imperial British East African Company was formed to develop this new interest, but it soon ran into financial troubles. The British government had to step in and take over the administration of the country. Despite this, they had little interest in Kenya, where the Masai and Nandi were fierce warriors. But Uganda was seen by Great Britain as a land of great potential.

THE RAILROAD

In 1896 Great Britain started to build a railroad to link Uganda to the Indian Ocean at Mombasa in Kenya. By 1899 the line had reached the site of modern-day Nairobi, and a small town quickly grew there. British farmers came to Kenya and settled along the railroad line. In 1900 there were an estimated 480 Europeans living in Kenya. By 1915 the number had grown to 5,000, and they had taken over large areas of land.

Reserves, usually on interior land, were set up for the displaced Africans, who were mainly Kipsikis, Masai, or Nandi. The Africans had no central government and could offer little opposition to the British and their modern weapons. When in 1905 the Nandi finally started to resist the British, they suffered brutal reprisals in which thousands were killed.

The years 1900 to 1914 were a period of increasing European influence in Africa. At the same time, the work of the missionaries brought Christianity to the country, and the missionary schools gave many Africans a Western education. Many of the young politicians who would soon start to fight for Kenyan independence studied at missionary schools.

HOLLYWOOD MOVIES SET IN AFRICA

Kenya's colonial history was for a time a favorite with Hollywood producers, who set a number of films in Africa. The movie that started this trend was Out of Africa, *a big-screen production filmed in 1985 that starred Meryl Streep and Robert Redford. The movie was based on the autobiography of Karen Blixen, a Dane who moved to Africa with her Swedish husband. Other Kenya-based movies have been less successful, such as the* Ghost and the Darkness *(1996), a movie about man-eating lions that interrupted the building of the railroad during the British colonial years.*

POLITICAL CHANGES

After World War I, Great Britain somewhat reluctantly took over the government of the former German area of Tanganyika (now Tanzania). This left them with an enormous East African empire. Many young British men, seeking a better life after serving in the army, immigrated to Kenya. In 1920 the country changed from a protectorate to a colony. Much of the highlands were reserved for European settlement, while Africans had to live in reserves. Africans were only allowed in the European settlements if they worked there, and identity cards were issued. Taxes were also imposed on the Africans in an attempt to force them into working on the plantations.

The war had changed the Africans' view of the Europeans. They had seen Europeans kill one another and found that this contradicted the message of the missionaries. At the same time, more Kenyans were emerging from the missionary schools with a Western education. The result was the formation of the first African political parties and the start of the independence movement.

UPRISING

Shortly after World War II, two Africans were appointed to the Legislative Council that governed Kenya. This was a sign of progress, although it was still not a fair enough representation to satisfy the growing demands of the Kenyans. In 1944 a new party called the Kenya African Union (KAU) was formed, and Jomo Kenyatta returned from England to lead the party. The KAU

AN AFRICAN HERO

Harry Thuku was the leader of the Young Kikuyu Association that later became the more militant East African Association. He led the group's protest against the lack of jobs and shrinking salaries in Kenya after World War I.

In March 1922 Thuku was arrested for political activity and remained in detention for 8 years. Thousands of people gathered in Nairobi to protest his arrest. Although noisy, the protesters were not armed, but the police became nervous about the large crowd and opened fire. In the confusion that followed, many people were killed—reports ranged from 20 to more than 100. Many more were injured. The massacre marked the start of the struggle for independence in Kenya.

was predominantly Kikuyu. The party campaigned for African independence and became involved in strikes and unrest that often threatened law and order.

In 1951, with their power growing, the KAU issued a five-point document of demands. When these were rejected, the stage was set for more violent protests. The following year, African freedom fighters started to slaughter European-owned cattle and murder Africans believed to support the European rulers. The resistance fighters became known as the Mau Mau. As a result, the European rulers declared a state of emergency. Jomo Kenyatta and other political leaders were arrested and imprisoned.

By 1953 the Europeans themselves became the target of attacks. Kenyatta was sentenced to 7 years imprisonment on charges of leading the Mau Mau. Over the next 3 years 32 European settlers were killed. In the same period, thousands of Kenyans, suspected of being part of the Mau Mau movement, died at the hands of government soldiers. The British were able to defeat the uprising with military force, but world opinion turned against them. Other African countries were gaining independence, and it was inevitable that Kenya would follow.

"Surely it cannot be necessary to go on killing these defenseless people on such an enormous scale."

—Winston Churchill, writing about the massacre of Africans between 1905 and 1908.

POSTINDEPENDENCE

Kenyatta led the Kenya African National Union (KANU) party to victory in the 1963 elections, and Kenya became independent on December 12 that year, with Kenyatta serving as the first prime minister. In 1974 Kenyatta was reelected to serve a third term in office, no surprise since by then the government had banned its main rival party, the Kenya People's Union (KPU). Regional tensions in the 1970s led to the East African Community's breakup, which did not help the Kenyan economy.

Daniel Taroitich arap Moi became president after Kenyatta's death in 1978 and made clear that he would not tolerate any opposition. The National Assembly passed laws to make KANU the only legal party, the press was more heavily censored, and the number of political prisoners increased.

In 1982 Kenya's stability was shattered when air force officers attempted a coup. There were several days of rioting before order was restored. In 1983 Moi was reelected for a second term, but he had no opponent. Students were now proving to be the president's most outspoken opponents, and for a while the University of Nairobi was closed.

In the same decade fighting in neighboring Sudan and Somalia threatened the stability of Kenya's own borders and brought many refugees into the country. Acquired immunodeficiency syndrome (AIDS) first appeared in Kenya in 1984 and became a major epidemic. Even the weather caused problems, and large areas of Kenya suffered a long drought that threatened millions of lives.

At the same time Western countries suspended aid to Kenya to pressure the country to return to multiparty politics and eliminate corruption. In December 1991 the Kenyan government gave in to external pressure and allowed other political parties to be formed. Mwai Kibaki's Democratic Party and Oginga Odinga's Forum for the Restoration of Democracy (FORD) emerged as the main rivals to KANU. However, the election in 1992 was marked by unrest, with two days of rioting in Nairobi. KANU won the election but it was seen by many to be unfair.

In August 1998 Kenya became the target of international terrorists when they bombed the U.S. embassy in Nairobi. In November 2002 an Israeli-

Jomo Kenyatta, a social activist and politician, became Kenya's first president and served from 1964 to 1978.

owned hotel in Mombasa was blown up, and there was an attempt to shoot down an Israeli charter airplane taking off from Mombasa airport with the use of two surface-to-air missiles.

As the 20th century came to a close, corruption and the misuse of government money meant that many Kenyans had a lower standard of living than ever before. It was clear that the people of Kenya were ready for change, and the 2002 elections saw KANU surrender power for the first time since independence. Moi handed over power to Mwai Kibaki in a peaceful transition that followed the The National Rainbow Coalition (NARC) victory over KANU in the December 2002 General Elections. In 2005 a proposed new constitution which was seen as a protest against President Kibaki was rejected by the voters. The president replaced his cabinet but some of the nominees rejected their appointments. The disputed presidential elections of 2007 resulted in violence and more than 1,100 deaths before the government and opposition came to a power-sharing agreement and agreed to a new cabinet.

After the March 2013 elections, Uhuru Kenyatta, the son of Jomo Kenyatta, was sworn in as Kenya's new president, where he proclaimed, "We will leave no community behind ... where there's disillusionment, we'll restore hope."

Ever since Kenya gained independence in 1963, Presidents Kenyatta and Moi ensured that the country maintained good relations with the West. Their legacy continues today, and the United Kingdom is Kenya's largest trade partner.

INTERNET LINKS

www.leakeyfoundation.org/

Official website of the Leakey Foundation for research related to human origins. The website contains links to information on the Leakey family, education, news, and events.

www.findagrave.com

This website is a searchable database of graves, cemeteries, and burial records of thousands of famous people from around the world. Type in the name John Hanning Speke for a link to his biography.

www.africanmeccasafaris.com

This website includes information on Kenya and has a link to the detailed history of Fort Jesus with many images.

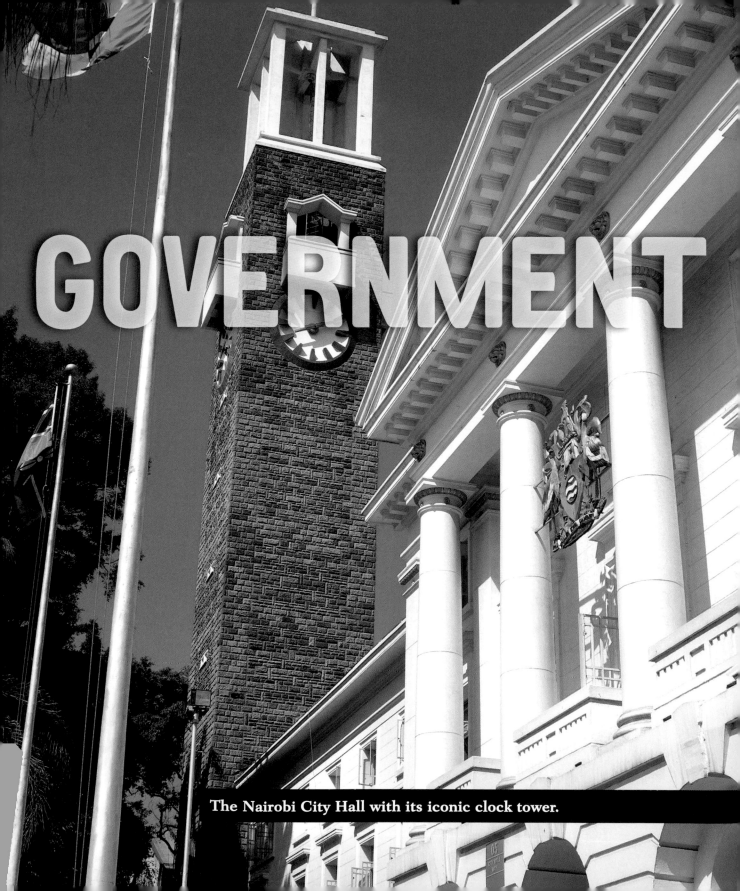

GOVERNMENT

The Nairobi City Hall with its iconic clock tower.

KENYA IS A DEMOCRATIC REPUBLIC whereby the president of Kenya is both head of state and head of government, and of a multiparty system. The new constitution of 2010 established a bicameral legislature. Details have yet to be finalized and will require significant legislative action. The country has close links with the West and is a member of the United Nations and the Commonwealth of Nations.

ELECTIONS

Elections are held every 5 years. The constitution of Kenya has three requirements for any candidate to be declared a winner: to get the largest number of votes among all contestants nationwide in absolute terms, to win at least 25 percent of the vote in at least five of Kenya's eight provinces, and to be elected member of parliament in a constituency. The Parliament of Kenya consists of the president and the National Assembly.

THE NATIONAL ASSEMBLY

Every 5 years Kenya holds elections to select the president and members of the National Assembly. All Kenyans 18 years of age and above are entitled to vote. The National Assembly consists of 290 members, each

3

A constitutional referendum was held in Kenya in 2010 and the new proposed constitution was promulgated on August 27, 2010, at a ceremony in Nairobi. On that day the new constitution, heralding the Second Republic, came into force.

The Parliament House in Nairobi. The motto over the main door of the building reads: "For a just society and the fair government of men."

elected by the registered voters of single member constituencies. Forty-seven members are women. Twelve members are nominated by parliamentary political parties according to their proportion of members in the National Assembly. These 12 people represent special interests including youth, disabled people, and workers. The Speaker is an ex officio member, that is, by virtue of his position.

After the election the president picks the cabinet and nominates the vice-president. The cabinet has about 20 members, and each member usually heads a department in the government.

THE SENATE

The Senate consists of 47 members each elected by registered voters, 16 women members who are nominated by political parties, 2 members representing the youth, 2 members representing the disabled, and the Speaker who is an ex officio member.

LOCAL GOVERNMENT

For administrative purposes Kenya is divided into eight provinces: Nyanza, Western, Rift Valley, Central, Eastern, North Eastern, Coast, and Nairobi. All the provinces are divided into districts, except for Nairobi. Each administrative division is headed by a provincial commissioner. The provinces are in turn divided into districts, each of which is headed by a district commissioner. All district and provincial commissioners are appointed by the president. They are responsible for areas such as education, health, and transportation. Provincial and district commissioners work alongside council departments, which are responsible for matters that include administration, finance, housing and social services, water and sewerage, and works and town planning.

Districts are further divided into divisions, headed by District Officers. Divisions consist of locations (headed by chiefs) and sub-locations (headed by sub-chiefs). Local authorities established under the Local Government Act are the city, municipal, county, town, county division, and urban councils.

Chiefs are powerful figures in their own community and are responsible for raising funds for health, transportation, and education. They might also mediate in disputes and supervise law and order. The chiefs and sub-chiefs have considerable day-to-day contact with the people in their area. They are expected to hold weekly meetings that are open to everyone where new laws and policies can be explained and local issues are discussed. These meetings are usually well attended and at this level the government is true democracy in action because they give everybody a chance to have a say in the running of their area.

THE PRESIDENT

JOMO KENYATTA The first president of Kenya, Kenyatta was born near Mount Kenya in 1894. He attended missionary school from 1909 to 1914 and was baptized Johnstone Kamau. He later worked for the Nairobi municipality and, after becoming involved in Kikuyu political groups, changed his name to Jomo Kenyatta.

By 1928 he had become general secretary of the Kikuyu Central Association (KCA). The following year he went to London to represent the organization. He made numerous speeches and pressured the British Parliament to grant Kenyans more say in running their own country. His work in England made Kenyatta famous back in his homeland, and he became a symbol of the Kenyan independence struggle.

Kenyatta returned to his country in 1930 but he had achieved only one of his goals: the right to develop independent educational institutions for Black Africans. In 1931 he returned to London to represent the KCA before a Parliamentary Commission on the Closer Union of East Africa. He stayed away from Kenya for the next 15 years, enrolling in the Moscow State University and later at the University College, London, where he studied social anthropology under the Polish anthropologist Bronislaw Malinowski. It

When Kenya was in its early years of nationhood, Kenyatta and his government sought to unite the diverse peoples of Kenya under the motto *harambee*, which means "pull together." When Moi took over as president, he used *nyayo* (n-YAH-yoh), or "follow the footsteps," as a slogan. The slogan expressed the respect Moi had for Kenyatta and stressed the values of peace, love, and unity among Kenyans.

The Kenyan national flag has three horizontal stripes separated by two narrow white bands. The black stripe represents the Kenyan people, the red symbolizes the struggle for independence, and the green stands for agriculture. The shield and spears in the center of the flag signify the defense of freedom.

The coat of arms bears two lions and the Swahili word harambee *(hah-rahm-BAY), which means "pull together." Harambee was a slogan used by President Kenyatta to unite the diverse peoples of Kenya.*

was during this time in England that Kenyatta wrote his thesis on Kikuyu culture and tradition that was published as *Facing Mount Kenya*, in 1938. Kenyatta continued to campaign for Kikuyu rights throughout his years in Great Britain where he lived throughout World War II. In 1946 he returned to Kenya and became president of the newly formed KAU in 1947. In the 1950s the colonial authorities suspected him of being involved with the Mau Mau uprising and imprisoned him. He was released in 1961 and helped KANU to victory in the 1963 election.

In 1963 Kenyatta became prime minister of independent Kenya. Soon after achieving independence, Kenya became a republic, and Kenyatta took the title of president. He was affectionately known as *Mzee* (m-ZAY), which can be translated as old one or wise one.

Throughout his rule, Kenyatta proved to be a conservative and tolerant leader, and Kenya became a moderate, stable, and pro-Western state. However, his greatest fear was that ethnic tensions would destroy the new country, and he used this as justification for ruthlessly destroying any political opposition.

Since 1967 Kenyatta's vice-president had been Daniel arap Moi. When Kenyatta died peacefully in his sleep on August 22, 1978, Daniel arap Moi took office as Kenya's second president.

DANIEL ARAP MOI   President Moi, a Kalenjin, was born in the Baringo district in 1924. He obtained his education at an African missionary school and worked as a schoolteacher from 1945 to 1957. At the same time he was involved in politics. Between 1948 and 1954 he served on the country's legislative council. He joined the cabinet in the early 1960s as minister of education. He went on to become minister of home affairs and in 1966 was elected vice-president. In 1978 he became president after Kenyatta died.

Moi was at first a popular president who was admired for his strong personality and intelligence. He became an influential figure in African politics and was voted chairperson of the Organization of African Union (OAU) for two consecutive terms in 1981 and 1982. Over the years, his failure to tackle Kenya's corruption problems became one of the main reasons why the country's economy started to falter. He began to lose popular support as a result, yet he became more determined than ever to retain power.

On the other hand, Moi was also a dignified and clever politician who was respected and consulted by many other African leaders. He was respectfully known as Father Moi to many Kenyans. In December 2002 Moi handed over power to Mwai Kibaki in a peaceful transition that followed the NARC victory over KANU in the 2002 General Elections.

MWAI KIBAKI   The 2002 elections clearly showed how much Kenyans yearned for change. Yet the man they elected, Mwai Kibaki, was not a new face, but one of the great veterans of Kenyan politics.

Kibaki was born in 1931 and became involved in Kenya's independence struggle after studying in Uganda and Great Britain. In 1963 Kibaki was elected to parliament and has been in politics ever since.

One of his greatest strengths is economics; he served as both finance minister and vice-president in the Moi government. When other parties were legalized in 1991, he resigned from KANU and founded the Democratic Party

Mwai Kibaki, a Kikuyu, was born on November 15, 1931. He graduated with a first-class honors degree in economics, history, and political science from the Makerere University in Uganda. He then studied at the London School of Economics on a scholarship. Kibaki was an assistant sales manager for an international oil company's Ugandan division and economics lecturer at the Makerere University before entering politics.

Opposite: From 1980, Daniel arap Moi's portrait graced the shilling, Kenya's currency for over 20 years.

Kenya's President-Uhuru Kenyatta speaking at the Catholic University in Nairobi in March 2013. Uhuru Kenyatta won the Kenya's presidential election with 50 percent of the vote but faces charges for crimes against humanity at the International Criminal Court for orchestrating the 2007 to 2008 post-election violence.

(DP). Kibaki ran against Moi in the 1992 and 1997 elections before being elected on his third attempt in 2002. His promises to Kenyans included an anti-corruption campaign, the reconstruction of the Kenyan economy, and the return of FPE. Kibaki is a Kikuyu, the largest ethnic group in Kenya.

The first year of NARC's rule proved difficult because of the fracturing of the NARC coalition. In 2005 Kibaki sacked his entire government and started with a new team that excluded all those who had voted against the new draft constitution he had proposed. Those who had voted against the draft formed a new party, Orange Democratic Movement-Kenya (ODM-Kenya). The elections in 2007 were bitterly fought but it was announced that Kibaki had won the Presidential race.

The opposition candidate Raila Odinga rejected the result. The European Union Election Observer Mission noted that the presidential elections fell short of international standards and lacked credibility. Kibaki's reelection met with communal violence. Rivalry between ethnic groups resulted in over 1,100 deaths and 60,000 people being displaced.

Kofi Annan, at the request of the African Union, led a panel to help negotiate a power-sharing deal between Odinga and Kibaki. In 2008 an agreement was signed and a Coalition Cabinet was sworn in with Raila Odinga as prime minister. A new constitution was approved in a referendum in 2010 that aimed for reforms that would prevent future contentious elections. In an interesting turn of events, Odinga had contested the results of the 2013 elections, which had been won by Uhuru Kenyatta, but the court ruled in Kenyatta's favor and he was sworn in as president in April 2013.

ETHNIC TENSION

One reason the European colonial powers gave for not granting Kenya independence was that the country's numerous ethnic groups would never be able to form a unified government.

Kenya's prisons suffer from serious overcrowding. In 2012 it was estimated that the total prison population was 52,000, including pretrial detainees and remand prisoners. These prisoners were in 99 prisons, and the official capacity of the entire prison system was 22,000 people. The occupancy level, based on official capacity, was 236.4 percent in February 2012. The number of prisoners grossly exceeds the maximum capacity of the prisons. The problem arises largely because people are detained for minor offenses, such as selling goods on the street without a license or brewing illegal alcohol. Yet there are very few other ways that poor Kenyans can earn some money.

Many detainees cannot afford bail, and because the legal system is slow, they may have to wait for months or even years before their cases are tried in courts.

In 1999 the Community Service Orders Program was introduced to alleviate overcrowding in Kenyan prisons. Under this program, minor offenders are allowed to stay in their own homes but have to perform community service for a specified period of time. However, the program has not succeeded in solving the problem, and prisons remain overcrowded. In addition Kenyan prisons commonly lack basic necessities such as water, food, and medical care. Prisoners are treated inhumanely and may be physically punished by prison officers.

The colonialists claimed that it was only their presence that kept Kenya from being ripped apart by warfare. This has proved to be mainly false. In the 40 years since independence, Kenya has been one of Africa's most stable nations.

Nevertheless, even Kenyan politicians acknowledge that ethnic differences still pose a danger. Kenyatta himself traveled to villages and hamlets preaching his message of *harambee*. Attempting to unite the country, he included influential people from other ethnic groups in his government.

Before the establishment of a national government, disputes within the community were usually settled at a gathering of the elders. For example, if somebody caused the accidental death of another person it was often the custom to pay a fine to the victim's family.

The modern Kenyan legal system still acknowledges the validity of traditional African customs in marriage, divorce, and matters affecting the family.

It might sound positive that the old "wise ways" are still respected. However, many women's groups are worried that women have few rights under the old traditions.

Oginga Odinga was made vice-president, and Tom Mboya was given a cabinet position. Both were Luos. Oginda Odinga was affiliated with the Forum for the Restoration of Democracy (FORD), the biggest organized political opposition group in Kenya, until his death in 1994. Tom Mboya, however, was murdered in Nairobi by a Kikuyu on July 5, 1969. Mboya's death led to ethnic tensions between the people of the Luo and Kikuyu communities.

Many people feel that it was only Kenyatta's personality that kept Kenya together. Although the transfer of power to Moi was peaceful, by 1992 clashes interfered with crop production when the violence spread to rural areas. Many died or were displaced from their homes. The fear of racial violence also began to affect the tourist trade.

THE LEGAL SYSTEM

Judicial authority is derived from the people. It is vested in, and exercised by, the courts and tribunals established by the constitution. The judiciary consists of the judges of the superior courts, magistrates' courts, and other judicial officers and staff. The Chief Justice is the head of the judiciary. The superior courts are the Supreme Court, the Court of Appeal, the High Court, and other courts established to hear and determine disputes relating to employment and labor relations, and the environment and land.

The Supreme Court is made up of the Chief Justice, the Deputy Chief Justice, and five other judges, and there must be five judges presiding in any proceeding. The Supreme Court has exclusive original jurisdiction to hear and determine disputes relating to the elections of the office of president and can hear appeals from the Court of Appeal and any other court or tribunal prescribed by national legislation.

The Court of Appeal must be made up of at least 12 judges. The president of the Court of Appeal is elected by the judges of the Court of Appeal from among themselves. The Court of Appeal has jurisdiction to hear appeals from the High Court. The High Court consists of a number of judges prescribed by an Act of Parliament. There is a Principal Judge of the High Court who is elected by the judges of the High Court from among themselves. The High Court has jurisdiction in criminal and civil matters.

The president appoints the Chief Justice and the Deputy Chief Justice subject to the approval of the National Assembly and all other judges in accordance with the recommendation of the Judicial Service Commission. Judges may retire at any time after reaching the age of 65 years, but has to retire by the age of 70 years. The Chief Justice may hold office for a maximum of 10 years.

The subordinate courts are the Magistrates' Courts, the Kadhis' Courts, the Courts' Martial, and any other court or tribunal established by an Act of Parliament. The jurisdiction of the Kadhis' Court is limited to questions of Muslim law relating to personal status, marriage, divorce, or inheritance in proceedings in which all parties profess the Muslim religion.

INTERNET LINKS

www.e-government.go.ke/
Official website of e-Government in Kenya.

www.information.go.ke/
The official ministry portal of the Government of Kenya, with information on the country and government services.

www.tommboya.org/
Official website of the Tom Mboya Foundation.

"Originally, the Africans had the land and the English had the Bible. Then the missionaries came to Africa and got the Africans to close their eyes and pray. And when they opened their eyes, the English had the land and the Africans had the Bible."
—Jomo Kenyatta, in response to the Europeans' argument that colonialism was good for Kenya.

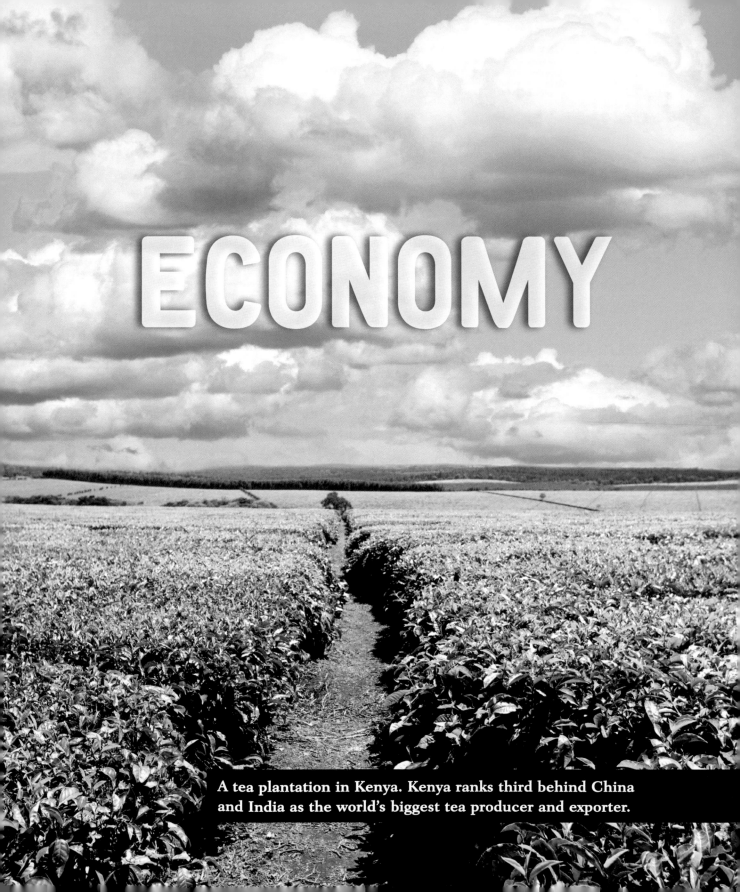

ECONOMY

A tea plantation in Kenya. Kenya ranks third behind China and India as the world's biggest tea producer and exporter.

4

KENYA WAS ONCE considered an economically successful country. Gross domestic product (GDP) grew at an annual average rate of 6.6 percent from 1963 to 1973. However, corruption and poor governance have taken a terrible toll on the nation's wealth. In the late 1990s and early 21st century, the declining economy suffered further blows.

The El Niño rains of 1997 and 1998 badly affected Kenyan farmers, while the 1998 bombing of the U.S. embassy in Nairobi had a negative impact on the tourist industry. In November 2002 an Israeli-owned hotel in Mombasa was bombed at the same time as an Arkia Airline airplane was the target of a missile launch at Mombasa airport. On September 21, 2013, a group of gunmen attacked the popular Westgate shopping mall in Nairobi, leading to a four-day gun battle with Kenyan armed forces, Islamic terrorist claimed responsibility for the attack, which resulted in 72 deaths and hundreds of injuries. Several countries including Great Britain and the United States have issued travel advisories warning their citizens not to visit parts of Kenya that are close to Somalia where most of the attacks have taken place. This made Kenya more dependent than ever on external financial aid.

Today the yearly income of the average Kenyan is around $730, while most of the population earns less than $1 a day. In addition, 40 percent of the population is unemployed, and half of all Kenyans live below the official poverty line.

Kenya has the largest economy in East Africa and has established itself as a regional hub for trade, finance, and transportation. Nairobi is the primary communication and financial hub of East Africa. Tea was Kenya's top export in 2010 accounting for $1.15 billion. Fresh horticulture exports fell from a record high of $1.12 billion in 2007 to $718 million in 2010. After the post-election violence of 2008 tourism dropped and then rebounded, bringing in $807 million in 2009. In 2010, the Kenyan Ministry of Tourism recorded nearly 1.1 million tourists and an 18 percent revenue growth in local currency terms.

Corn, or maize, is a popular food choice. Usually paired with beans.

The Kenyan economy is centered on agriculture. Around 75 percent of employed Kenyans cultivate the land. Tea, coffee, and horticulture produce approximately half of the nation's exports. Much of the land is divided into small plots for subsistence farmers. Each farmer produces just enough food for the family and perhaps a little more to sell in the local market. Corn, cassava, sweet potatoes, and fruit, such as coconut and pineapple, are the main subsistence crops.

SMALL-SCALE FARMING

Subsistence farmers have been encouraged to grow crops to sell. Farmers living in the highlands often grow a few coffee plants. By the end of the 1990s two-thirds of the coffee, nearly half the tea, and all the sugarcane produced in Kenya came from small-scale farmers. Farmers use the money obtained from these cash crops to buy tools, lamps, blankets, and clothing.

The main crops grown in this way are corn, millet, sweet potatoes, cassava, potatoes, and fruits, such as passion fruit, mangoes, pineapples, coconuts, and bananas. Of these, corn is the most important and the staple diet of many Kenyans. A typical farmer owns about one to three acres. His land may even be "fragmented," consisting of several tiny and separate plots. Often, he will be able to afford only the most basic tools, and most of the work will have to be done by hand. The standard of living of the rural community remains low.

The government helps farmers by paying for fertilizer, insecticide, or new strains of seed. Officials also visit the villages to introduce new farming techniques, advise about pest control, or plan irrigation projects. Traditionally, a farmer would divide his land among his sons. However, with Kenya's growing population, there is often not enough land to support everyone. Many young men have been forced to leave their homes to seek work in the cities.

Small-scale farming remains the largest employment opportunity for women in Kenya, who form the bulk of the workforce, estimated at 82 percent, according to the World Bank. The income generated here pays for food, education, and medicine.

CASH CROPS

Agriculture accounts for 26 percent of Kenya's GDP, and farming for export is vital to the country's economy. Coffee and tea are two of the more important crops. Both are grown in the fertile highland region, where there are many large plantations.

Diversifying the economy has become more important because the world price for coffee fluctuates. Tea growing has increased to offset the decline in coffee prices. High-quality Kenyan tea is particularly popular in Europe, but Kenyan tea has to compete with cheaper tea produced in Asian countries.

In recent years growing fresh vegetables, fruit, and flowers for export has become Kenya's fastest-growing industry. In 2011 horticultural exports contributed 11 percent of GDP. Europe purchases 90 percent of Kenya's horticultural products.

An employee packing roses for export in Naivasha.

HORTICULTURE In the past 20 years, growing flowers, fruits, and vegetables for markets in Europe has become big business in Kenya. Kenyan goods that you will find in European supermarkets include cut flowers, French beans, runner beans, snow peas, and fruits, such as pineapples, mangoes, and passion fruit. The Kenyan climate is excellent for growing such produce, labor is cheap, and Nairobi airport can provide frequent flights to Europe. As a result Kenyan products have been praised for their high quality.

Flowers, such as roses, have become the symbol of the industry and in a good year 38,000 tonnes of Kenyan flowers can be sent to Europe.

The horticulture industry has expanded with little help from the government, and although there are many farms owned by big companies, much of the produce comes from smallhold farmers. It has been estimated that up to a quarter of a million households in Kenya are able to subsidize their

Flower farms near Lake Naivasha in the Great Rift Valley. Flowers such as roses, carnations, and lilies are grown under automated greenhouses.

incomes by growing produce for the export market. This is one reason why the Kenyan horticulture industry has been held up as an excellent example of how other African countries might organize similar projects.

However, there have also been problems. Many people claim that the small-scale growers are paid too little for their produce and are being exploited by middlemen or the European supermarkets. Some of the suppliers respond by accusing the smallhold growers of being unreliable and often failing to supply the goods they have promised, or not producing goods of a sufficiently high quality. Experts brought in to help small farmers found that on one farm the workers were sorting their vegetables by laying them on the ground where they became contaminated by bacteria and so were rejected by the European buyers. Giving the workers some tables on which to sort the produce solved this problem.

An agribusiness model where companies are contracting smallholder farmers to supply food and beverage raw materials for processing is emerging. This has the potential to stop the poverty cycle driven by the middlemen who take up to a third of farmers' sales. East Africa Breweries and Coca Cola aim to contract some smallhold farmers in 2012. The project should result in higher income for small-scale farmers, who have sometimes lacked motivation for commercial farming because of lack of market or extremely low prices for seasonal produce when there is oversupply. The Coca Cola project is expected to benefit 50,000 small-scale farmers growing mangoes and passion fruits. It is being implemented through a development group with funding from the Bill and Melinda Gates Foundation. Farmers will be helped and encouraged to increase yields and improve standards of quality control.

COFFEE

The coffee plant is an evergreen shrub that grows best at higher altitudes. In the wild it can grow up to 32.8 feet (10 m) tall, but on plantations it is usually pruned much shorter to make harvesting easier. Coffee plants did not grow in the wild in Kenya, but were introduced by the Europeans. A good coffee plant will produce about one and a half pounds of roasted coffee each year. It takes between 3 and 4 years to bear fruit, and then produces coffee for 20 to 30 years.

The coffee tree produces a berry called a coffee cherry that changes from green to yellow and finally, when it is ripe, to bright red. A coffee bean is actually the seed of the cherry-like fruit. The berries ripen at different speeds. At harvest time, teams of pickers move along the rows of plants, removing the red beans but leaving the others. This careful method of picking is one reason why Kenyan coffee is considered to be of such high quality.

After being harvested, the berries are taken to the sorting yard where the sacks are emptied and any leaves, twigs, or green berries are removed. The berries are then placed in a pulping machine where the flesh is stripped from the fruit. Each berry has two beans (seeds) and these are covered in a second skin. The beans are either left in the sun to dry as pulped natural coffee or they are left in fermenting tanks for 16 to 36 hours to loosen the remaining husks. They are then washed and spread out to dry. At the drying racks, workers smooth the wet husks into a single layer so that they can dry properly. Following this process, the crop is sent to Nairobi. Here, the berries are extracted from the last of the husks and then sent to be auctioned.

The East African Breweries project involves the growing of sorghum. Government policies had discouraged the growing of sorghum in favor of corn and beans. But sorghum, unlike beans and corn, can grow in semiarid areas and is one of the crops that is considered drought-resistant. Kenyan Agricultural Research Institute (KARI) scientists have estimated that 70 percent of Kenya cannot grow corn as former growing areas are turning into semiarid areas conducive to growing sorghum. It is projected that 10,000 farmers will benefit from this project. They are being offered low interest loans to buy seed as well as technical support. East Africa Malting is investing in sorghum as a malting substitute.

INDUSTRY

A worker prepares parts of leather, which would eventually be manufactured into handbags, at a stall in Nairobi.

Kenya has relatively little industry, with manufacturing only accounting for 16.4 percent of the economy. The lack of industry means Kenya has to import many items, such as machinery and transportation equipment. Kenyan factories produce consumer goods, including plastics, textiles, and soap for the local market.

A great deal of work also goes on in small-scale workshops called *jua kali* (joo-AH KAH-lee), which employ small numbers of people to make simple items from metal or wood. *Jua kali* means hot sun in Kiswahili and was originally used to describe people who worked outdoors and could fix practically anything upon request.

ENERGY

More than 60 percent of Kenya's energy comes from hydroelectric power plants. There are dams on the Tana River and in the Turkwel River Gorge. Hydroelectric power is dependent on the rain, so droughts in recent years have caused serious interruptions in the electrical supply.

Geothermal energy is generated using natural steam tapped from volcanic active zones in the Rift Valley. Thermal (fuel generated) energy is

AN EXAMPLE OF HOW CORRUPTION WORKS

The government has funds for a big construction project, and three construction companies submit tenders. The government officials supervising the project do not pick the best company to do the job, but the one offering them the biggest bribe.

Having paid a bribe to get the project, the construction company has less money to do the work. Its own directors might also take a share of the contract money. Since the government officials in charge of supervising the project have already taken their share, they do not interfere with the graft of the company directors.

The project has to be built cheaply, so substandard materials and poor construction techniques are used. The government should refuse to accept the low-quality work, but inspections are done by the same government officials who took the bribe. They accept the work, and two years later the building begins to fall apart. Newspapers report the problem. The officials responsible should get in trouble, yet this seldom happens. The case is dismissed in court if it gets there at all, and the people involved remain unpunished.

generated in power stations in Mombasa and Nairobi. Kenya Electricity Generating Company (KenGen) produces about 80 percent of Kenya's electricity consumed in the country. Electricity is produced from various sources, including hydro, geothermal, thermal, and wind.

Kenya does not have any oil, but it refines imported oil in Mombasa and then sells it to other African countries.

TOURISM

In 1986 tourism overtook coffee as Kenya's number one source of foreign income. Money had been invested in hotels, and the Kenya Utalii College in Nairobi trained young Kenyans to work in the industry. With wildlife-rich game parks and beautiful beaches, the tourist industry seemed set to expand further.

However, tourism is a sensitive industry, and events such as the 1998 bombing of the U.S. embassy in Nairobi and a general increase in crime have led to a drastic drop in the number of visitors.

Tourists flock to Kenya during the annual wildebeest migration period to witness the natural spectacle unfold.

The year 2002 was expected to be the start of a general recovery, but hopes were dashed by more terrorist attacks, this time in Mombasa aimed at a tourist hotel and an airplane on take-off from the airport. These attacks happened within minutes of each other.

The war in Iraq in 2003 renewed fears about safety, especially among Americans, many of whom opted not to travel overseas. During the period of heightened security against terrorist activities, the U.S. and British embassies in Kenya closed several times. The United States, Great Britain, and other Western countries also advised against travel to Kenya after a number of their citizens were kidnapped or murdered in 2011. The number of tourists arriving by cruise ship in 2012 dropped dramatically due to insecurity and pirates in the Indian Ocean. These factors, along with the 2013 mall attack, produced a sharp decline in Kenya's tourist arrivals and its tourism-generated revenue.

The decreasing number of tourists also affects environment-friendly ventures. Ecotourism provides the framework and means to support wildlife conservation projects in Kenya and involves people who live alongside wildlife, as they get a certain percentage from ecotourism revenues. Such mutually beneficial programs, however, are in danger of being abandoned if tourist arrivals continue to decline.

GOVERNMENT CORRUPTION AND INEFFICIENCY

A major economic problem in Kenya is government corruption and inefficiency. The government wholly or partly owns many companies, from factories to banks. In charge of such organizations are politicians, some with little business experience and some corrupt officials.

Billions of Kenyan shillings were in the past poured into wholly or partly government-owned organizations. Often the money seemed to disappear, when it could have been used to fund road repairs, the building of schools and hospitals, the improvement of the telephone service, and other projects to improve the living standard of Kenyans.

Many problems that hamper business in Kenya today are the result of government corruption and inefficiency. Kenya is taking steps to check the problem by gradually privatizing organizations that are partly or wholly owned by the government. Telkom Kenya, Kenya Ports Authority, Kenya Railways Corporation (KRC), National Cereals and Produce Board (NCPB), Kenya Commercial Bank, and Kenya Reinsurance Corporation are some such organizations that have been or are being privatized.

The Kenyan civil service is also known to be too large. It adds to the waste of government money. In addition, many civil servants do not get paid much, so they augment their salaries by accepting bribes.

During former President Kibaki's administration, a number of former heads of partly or wholly government-owned companies have been charged in anti-corruption courts for misconduct and abuse of power while they were in office. Current President Kenyatta is also pursuing a strong anti-corruption policy.

INTERNET LINKS

www.kenyacoffee.or.ke/

Official website of the Kenya Coffee Traders Association that includes information on growing coffee in Kenya.

www.coffeeresearch.org/

Website with a wealth of information about coffee, including sections on history, agriculture, science, politics, and the market. There are links to images and videos.

www.trust.org

This website has a link to an informative article entitled Anti-corruption profile—Kenya.

ENVIRONMENT

Sunflowers grow in a field in the Great Rift Valley.

5

THE NATIONAL ENVIRONMENT Management Authority (NEMA) is a government organization that has been established to supervise and coordinate all matters relating to the environment in Kenya.

It is the principal instrument of government in the implementation of policies relating to the environment and its mission is to safeguard and enhance the quality of the environment through coordination, research, and enforcement while encouraging participation toward sustainable development.

Kenya is famous for its game reserves. The Masai Mara, with open grass plains where zebras, giraffes, and elephants roam in large numbers, is what many people would consider typical Africa. People from around the world visit Kenya for safari holidays, and tourism makes an important contribution to the economy.

The government is committed to preserving the country's natural heritage. However, there are serious problems that threaten the future of Kenya's wildlife.

A HISTORY OF KENYAN WILDLIFE

Before the Europeans started to colonize Africa, the continent's animals lived in harmony with the people. Whether this was because the people had a natural understanding of nature or simply lacked the technology to have any great impact on the environment is debatable.

The National Environment Management Authority (NEMA) is a government organization that has been established to supervise and coordinate all matters relating to the environment. It is the principal instrument of government in the implementation of policies relating to the environment and its mission is to safeguard and enhance the quality of the environment through coordination, research, and enforcement while encouraging participation toward sustainable development.

COLONIAL AFRICA The arrival of European colonists in the 15th century signaled the start of environmental destruction, particularly in the south of the continent where widespread and indiscriminate hunting almost eliminated the big game.

By the turn of the 20th century a few people started to realize that Africa's wildlife needed to be conserved and protected. The permission to hunt was limited to people with licenses, and most of Kenya's game parks were established in the period between 1945 and 1960. The game parks were generally restricted to dry areas that were expensive to farm but nevertheless provided refuge for wildlife. Most of the first game wardens were European, and the parks were often established with little thought for the local people. The Masai, for example, lost vital dry season water holes. This created conflicts that continue today even though it is acknowledged that the area is a reserve rather than a national park, and it belongs to the Masai people.

POSTINDEPENDENCE When Kenya became independent in 1963 nobody was sure what the new government's attitude to the country's wildlife would be, but the government was quick to see the value of tourism and continued to maintain the game parks. In 1977 the government banned hunting safaris as well as the sale of skins, horns, and other animal trophies. It was a brave step as hunting safaris traditionally generated a lot of money. The 1970s and 1980s were bad times for Kenyan wildlife. Political corruption and a declining economy left the game department short of funds, and poaching increased and became more violent. At the same time huge areas of the country were struck by drought. The two factors combined to drastically reduce Kenya's rhinoceros and elephant populations. According to the African Conservation Foundation, 70 percent of Kenya's wildlife outside national parks has been poached out. Kenya's African elephant (*Loxodonta africana spp.*) plummeted by 85 percent between 1973 and 1989. Black rhinoceroses (*Diceros bicornis*) decreased in number from 20,000 in 1970 to 350 by 1983. It remains on the IUCN Red List of Threatened Species as critically endangered, although recent success in black rhino conservation is encouraging.

Unrest in neighboring countries, particularly Somalia, added to the problem. In 1989 the famous conservationist George Adamson, protector of lions and their environment, was killed by poachers in Kenya. It was a turning point. The Kenya Wildlife Service (KWS) was established, and Richard Leakey headed the organization from 1989 to 1994. Wardens received better training and the KWS introduced a shoot-to-kill policy with poachers. Leakey also fought corruption within the service. President Moi highlighted the government's commitment by publicly burning Kenya's stockpile of ivory. Although the measures helped, it was a worldwide ban on ivory trading in 1989 that helped to reduce elephant poaching in Kenya.

A black rhinoceros at the Lake Nakuru Nature Reserve.

In 2002 Michael Wamithi, a highly respected young Kenyan with years of experience in conservation work, became director of the KWS. Under his guidance the KWS reduced park entrance fees for Kenyans and launched an advertising campaign to attract local people to their country's game parks. Julius Kipng'etich was appointed director of KWS in 2005. He has given conservation a strong scientific approach while continuing to improve the management of the parks. In 2012 Kipng'etich resigned his directorship and William Kibet Kiprono was appointed director.

IVORY BAN

Before the ivory ban, countries could sell elephant tusks that had been collected legally. This included ivory collected by game wardens from elephants that had died of natural causes. There was a big demand for ivory in Asia, where it was carved into ornaments, and people argued that the government should be able to use money from ivory sales to help support the game parks.

Elephant tusks are more valuable than ever before, especially in Asia. Due to the soaring demand in the black market, poachers have become increasingly ruthless in obtaining them.

Unfortunately some corrupt government officials were willing to issue false paperwork. That made it easy for poaching syndicates to export tusks disguised as legal ivory to the Far East. Burundi, for example, exported tons of ivory from 1976 to 1986, yet there were hardly any elephants in the country. The ivory was believed to have come from elephants killed by poachers in other East African countries.

The 1989 Convention on International Trade in Endangered Species (CITES) introduced a total ban on ivory sales throughout the world. There was no longer such a thing as legal ivory, and tusks discovered by customs anywhere around the world could be seized. That quickly and drastically reduced elephant poaching.

In 2002 CITES members approved conditional one-time sales of stock-piled ivory in Botswana, Namibia, and South Africa. This ivory was theoretically sourced from elephants that had died naturally or had been culled. The sale took place in 2008. After the stockpile sale took place Environment Investigation Agency (EIA) investigations revealed that flooding the market with legal ivory had not reduced demand. Approximately 90 percent of the ivory on sale had come from illegal sources, and the market value of illegal ivory had increased dramatically. In 2010 Tanzania and Zambia petitioned for special permission to hold another sale of stockpiled ivory. Permission was refused by CITES. Any legal trade in elephant ivory incentivizes elephant poaching and illegal ivory sales.

CONSERVATION IN KENYA

Kenyan wildlife is managed and protected by the KWS. There are also a number of conservation groups working on different projects. The OSIENALA, or Friends of Lake Victoria, are an NGO based in the region. They focus on issues affecting fisherfolk around the lake. In collaboration with their international partner, the Global Nature Fund, they provide water-purification systems for schools in the area to ensure a clean water supply

CHOKED LAKE VICTORIA

The water hyacinth (Eichhornia crassipes) is among the world's most invasive weeds. Native to the tropics of South America it was introduced in Africa around 1879 and by 1989 had established itself in Lake Victoria. By 1998 it was estimated to have covered about 77 square miles (199.4 square km) of the lake's surface. The mat of vegetation is so thick that fishermen cannot launch their boats into the water. Native aquatic plants cannot get the light they need because sunlight cannot filter through the plants to the water below. This affects the well-being of native fish and other animals in the lake. The plants impede waterflow making the lake stagnant and allowing mosquitos to breed.

The water hyacinth problem was brought under control with aggressive removal methods and by the release of an insect, the Neochetina weevil, that killed the plant by eating the leaves. The weevil also burrows into the stalks, destroying them so that the plant rots and dies. By 2005 aerial photographs showed the lake to be clear.

In 2006 unusually heavy rains raised the water level of the lake and swept nutrient-rich sediment into the water. The influx of nutrients and fertilizer from agricultural run-off encouraged a fresh outbreak of water hyacinth.

The problem of water hyacinth in Lake Victoria and restoring the lake's health is now an international mission, with the World Bank allocating $77 million to a range of programs to control the invasive weed and reestablish a sustainable fishing industry.

and reduce the risk of water-borne diseases. Other projects have included planting trees to promote smallholder tree farming. Conservation groups, such as TRAFFIC, the wildlife trade monitoring network, work to ensure that trade in wildlife is legal. It is a world organization with branches in the country. Kenyan individuals have also contributed to conservation. Michael Werikhe, nicknamed the Rhino Man, was an early pioneer of conservation. He has walked thousands of miles on different continents, educating people about the plight of the rhinoceros and how close it is to extinction. The money he has raised has gone toward rhino conservation programs. In 1990 Werikhe was awarded the Goldman Environmental Prize, the world's largest prize honoring grassroots environmentalists. Wangari Maathai was awarded the

Nobel Peace Prize in 2004 and is internationally recognized for her persistent struggle for democracy, human rights, and environmental conservation. She is famous for her conservation work. Through the Green Belt Movement she has helped women to plant more than 20 million trees on farms, schools, and church compounds in order to conserve the environment.

ENDANGERED WILDLIFE

The African Fund for Endangered Wildlife Kenya Ltd (AFEW (K) Ltd) is a nonprofit organization. It is also known as the Giraffe Centre and was founded in 1979 by the late Jock Leslie-Melville. His vision was to create an educational establishment in conjunction with rescuing the endangered Rothschild giraffe. Its main objective is to provide conservation education for school children and the youth of Kenya. All education programs are offered free of charge.

GAME PARKS There are over 40 wildlife reserves and national parks in Kenya that have been set aside for the conservation of natural habitat and wildlife. Many of these areas offer visitors a chance to see animals in their natural habitat in the unspoilt wilderness of remote parts of Kenya. Safari camps have been established in the parks and knowledgeable guides are available to take visitors on excursions into the countryside.

PROBLEMS AHEAD

GROWING POPULATION Despite efforts to protect Kenya's wildlife, the next decade could be difficult. One of the greatest problems is Kenya's growing population. Nature reserves and game parks, that have been set aside for wildlife habitats, are becoming more crowded as the human population increases and settlements spill over into these areas. A good example is Nairobi National Park. The area is vital to wildlife as water can be found there in the dry season. Although the park is protected, human settlements along the rivers outside the parks make it increasingly difficult for the animals to move across their old routes to reach the water.

The close proximity of human residences and wildlife habitats has created other problems. Animals such as elephants and zebras raid nearby farms when they run out of food or when the rivers are dry. Hippopotamuses and crocodiles pose a serious danger to villagers who have to go to the rivers to collect water or wash clothes. These animals sometimes kill people who get in their way and themselves get killed by people who either fear them or are angry with them for the destruction they cause.

A warden briefs an anti-poaching patrol at Tsavo West National Park, whose job involves removing snares and identifying the location of poachers.

GLOBAL WARMING The African environment is badly affected by global warming. Kenya, which does not contribute very much to global warming, might be one of the countries that suffers the most. Much of the country is semiarid land that is prone to drought and is therefore extremely vulnerable to any climatic changes.

POACHING The number of mammals throughout Kenya is falling partly because of poaching for food, and the meat is known as bushmeat. In February 2003 environmental teams found 200 snares in Tsavo National Park in just one day. Over 1,000 snares were found in the first month and the teams also caught a poacher with 19 dead Dik-diks. There are thousands of snares in each of Kenya's national parks, and the snares trap any animal that happens to come along. In one search of the Masai Mara Reserve in 2001 a poacher's camp was found. Over 20 people had been camping there and the camp had many dead animals: eight hippos, eight eland, a leopard, elephant tusks, and full drying racks for meat. Apart from people who poach to feed their families, there are also those who catch as many animals as they can to profit from bushmeat sales in local and international markets.

THREATENED FLORA AND FAUNA   The endangered African wild dogs (*Lycaon pictus*) are hunted by farmers and cattle herders who fear that they will attack goats and other domestic animals. The expanding human population has resulted in settlements that intrude on the wild dogs' habitats. This leads to contact between the wild dogs and domestic animals and causes the wild dogs to contract diseases such as distemper. Today the estimated population of the African wild dog is less that 5,500 throughout sub-Saharan Africa.

Rhinos have been driven to near extinction. The world rhino population has fallen by more than 90 percent in the last 30 years. The species that still exist in Africa are the black rhinoceros (*Diceros bicornis*) and white rhinoceros (*Ceratotherium simum*). The Ngulia Rhino Sanctuary in Kenya is a haven for rhinos. The aim is to allow them to breed without the threat of poachers and ultimately to rebuild the population and reintroduce them into the wild. From three rhinos in 1986, Ngulia is now home to more than 70 individuals protected by an electric fence.

The African wild dog is a highly social and intelligent animal. The African Wild Dog Conservation (AWDC) has been carrying out research to provide a threat assessment and management plan for these dogs.

In 2011 a new population of Africa's most critically endangered forest antelope was discovered by scientists using hidden cameras. Aders' duiker (*Cephalophus adersi*), a very rare small forest antelope, was found living in the threatened Boni-Dodori forest in northern Kenya. The images from the camera also showed populations of African wild dogs, elephants (*Loxodonta africana*), and lions (*Panthera leo*), living in and around the biodiverse forest, that is currently under threat from rapid coastal and agricultural development. In 2010 a new species of giant sengi, also known as an elephant shrew (*Macroscelidea*), was found in the same area. Kenyan forests are particularly vulnerable. They now cover a very small area, and the Moi government has been accused of allocating portions of the forest to building developers or to landless people in exchange for votes. Yet the rainforests are vital habitat for many animals, some of which are only now being discovered. The forests also help to stabilize the weather as they attract rain and the tree root systems help to control flooding. Forests are also needed for the survival of the tea industry. Tea plantations are usually located next to forests as the trees provide shade from extreme weather and bring microclimatic benefits to the soil.

UNREST IN NEIGHBORING COUNTRIES Kenya borders Somalia, where there is very little law and order, and armed bandits sometimes operate in the Kenyan game parks. Some gangs come across the border, while others could be from refugee camps within Kenya. Game wardens have been killed by Somalian poachers, while visitors run a risk of being robbed or attacked, especially in some of the more remote game parks.

INTERNET LINKS

www.nema.go.ke/
Official website of the National Environment Management Authority (NEMA) in Kenya, with detailed information on environmental issues, including pollution, waste management, education, and natural resource management.

www.nairobinationalpark.wildlifedirect.org/2010/08/09/history-of-kenyas-oldest-national-park/
The Wildlife Direct website has information on Nairobi National Park as well as links to images of some of the animals found in the park.

www.osienala.org/
Official website of OSIENALA (Friends of Lake Victoria), an NGO that operates within the Lake Victoria basin and focuses on issues affecting the fisherfolks around the lake.

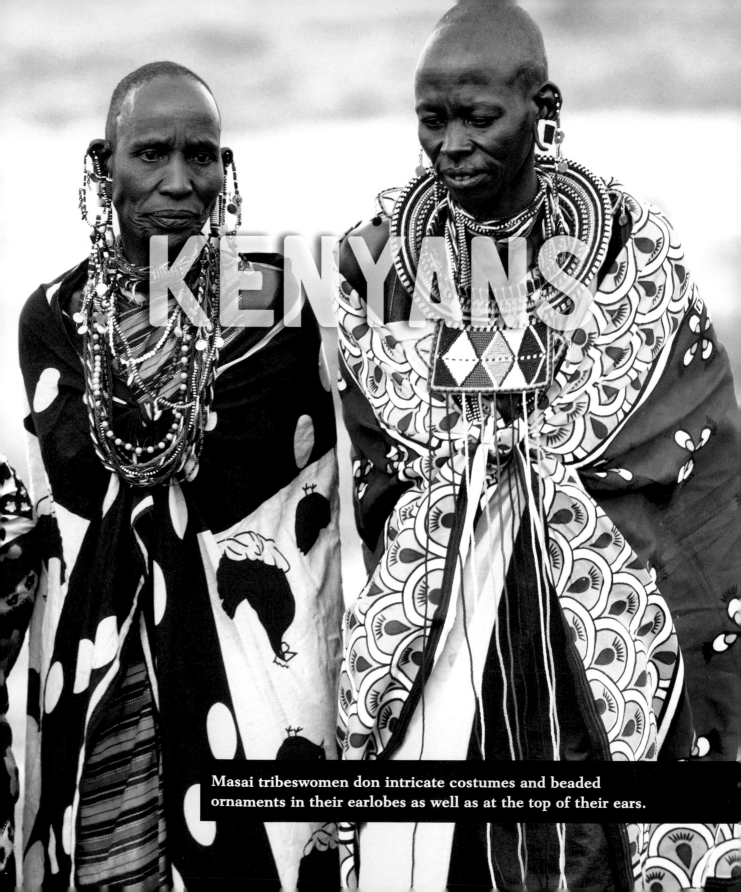

KENYANS

Masai tribeswomen don intricate costumes and beaded ornaments in their earlobes as well as at the top of their ears.

KENYA'S BORDERS WERE CREATED by its European colonial rulers with no regard to the geographical distribution of languages or ethnic groups. The largest group is the Kikuyu, which has about 6.5 million members. The smallest group is the El Molo, with fewer than 500 people. El Molo people live in villages on the southeastern shore of Lake Turkana. Their main diet is fish from the lake.

Fishermen from the El Molo tribe use a raft and handmade harpoons to catch fish from Lake Turkana.

6

Approximately 99 percent of Kenya's population of 43 million people is of African descent. That group is composed of 70 different ethnic groups. The largest ethnic group is the Kikuyu, accounting for 22 percent of the population of African descent. Other significant groups are the Luhya, Luo, Kalenjin, Kamba, Kisii, and Meru. Asians, Europeans, and Arabs account for 1 percent of the population.

In other parts of Africa such diversity has led to serious political problems and even ethnic violence. Kenyatta's government was aware of this danger and worked to build a postindependence national identity under the motto *harambee*, or pull together. This has not always been successful. Most politicians have been accused at some point of favoring people from their own ethnic groups. Compared with other African countries, however, Kenyans have managed to get along relatively well.

CLASSIFYING PEOPLE

A person can be identified as coming from a certain ethnic group by their physical appearance, the clothes they wear, the food they eat, the way they speak, and many other factors. Masai men walking down the streets of Nairobi may stand out because of their clothes. Of course, many Masai who live in Nairobi often wear Western-style clothes, but another Kenyan will still recognize them as being Masai if they are speaking in Maa, which is the Masai language. If the Masai wear Western-style clothes and speak in Kiswahili or English, many people will still be able to identify them from their height, accent, or perhaps the way their ears are pierced.

The main tool scientists use to classify ethnic groups is language. Indigenous Kenyans are categorized into three main groups: Bantu, Cushites, and Nilotes. These groups are then further classified according to their own specific languages.

THE MAIN BANTU GROUPS

Bantu is a linguistic term that refers to people who speak Bantu languages. The Bantu make up about 65 percent of the population. Examples of Bantu groups in Kenya include the Abaluhya of western Kenya, the Kikuyu of central Kenya, and the Meru, Embu, and Kamba of the eastern parts of Kenya. The Bantu originally came from West and Central Africa. On arriving in Kenya they occupied the upper regions around Lake Victoria, central Kenya, and the southern coastal area. The early Bantu were mainly farmers.

The single largest group in Kenya is the Kikuyu with about 22 percent of the total population. The Kikuyu moved into the area around Mount Kenya between the 17th and 19th centuries. They were among the first to have contact with the Europeans and among the first to lose their land to European farmers. The Kikuyu were also some of the first Kenyans to accept Western education and modern ideas. As a result of that they became one of the most influential groups in modern Kenyan society.

The Kamba migrated to the dry land between Nairobi and the coast and became cattle herders and traders. They are noted for their skillful wood carvings and significant contributions to modern Kenyan music.

The Luhya come from the heavily populated western part of the country, although many have moved to Nairobi and elsewhere to seek work. The Luhya are traditionally noted for their pottery and basket weaving. Like other Kenyans, Luhyas are today found in almost every sector of the Kenyan economy. They practice farming and agriculture in their native western Kenya region where they grow sugarcane and other cash crops.

A group of Kikuyu boys perform the tribal dance in school. Dancing is seen as a symbol of power constituting of the integration of momentum, cognitive energy, force of gravity, and muscularity.

A Masai woman herds goats. Herders usually have to travel long distances in search of food for the animals.

The Meru migrated to the northeastern side of Mount Kenya in the 14th century. The name Meru refers to both the location and people. Living on good farmland, the Meru produce much of Kenya's tea and coffee.

The Swahili are different from the other Bantu peoples. The term Swahili refers to a people as well as culture. Although they speak a Bantu language, their culture comes from Africans and Arabs living together over many centuries. Their shipbuilding technology, skills as ocean traders, long adoption of the Islamic faith, architecture, and way of dressing all distinguish them from other Kenyans.

THE MAIN NILOTIC GROUPS

The term Nilotic is linguistic and originates from the term Nile. The Nilotic peoples originated in the Nile Valley and migrated to Kenya about 600 years ago. While the Bantu people are believed to have arrived from the West, the Nilotic people came from the North. In Kenya, Nilotes are divided into three main groups.

The Highland Nilotes are also referred to as the Kalenjin speakers. The Nani, the Kipsigis, and Pokot are Highland Nilotes, they are found in the Rift Valley. The Kalenjin settled in the Great Rift Valley in 1500. Originally thought to be pastoralists, many are now farmers. The Kipsikis, Nandi, Tugen, and Elgeyo are all subgroups of the Kalenjin. About 75 percent of Kenya's great runners are Kalenjin. Former Kenyan president Moi is a Kalenjin from the Tugen subgroup.

THE BIGGEST TRIBES

By language group

Bantus: 65 percent

Nilotes: 31 percent

Cushites: 4 percent

By tribe

Kikuyu: 22 percent (Bantu)

Luhya: 14 percent (Bantu)

Luo: 13 percent (Nilote)

Kalenjin: 12 percent (Nilotes)

Kamba: 11 percent (Bantu)

Kisii: 6 percent (Bantu)

Meru: 6 percent (Bantu)

Other Africans: 15 percent

Asians, Europeans, and Arabs: 1 percent

The Plain Nilotes include the Masai and they are found in the Rift Valley, the Iteso of western Kenya, and the Turkana of northern Kenya. River Lake Nilotes include the Luo who live around Lake Victoria. Today most Nilotes are farmers, including some sectors of the Masai. Only the Tutkana are mainly pastoralists in present-day Kenya. The Luo and Turkana also practice fishing. The Luo were traditionally herders, but many settled around Lake Victoria and became fisherfolk. Others found their new home more suitable to farming. Like the Kikuyu the Luo have successfully adapted to modern Kenyan society, and many have become mechanics, machinists, and traders. As a result the Luo are a powerful force in the trade unions. They also took a leading role in the independence struggle. The Luo won political influence when Oginga Odinga, a Luo, became vice-president of Kenya in 1963.

The Masai are a distinctive ethnic group that many people living outside Kenya can recognize. Their ancestors migrated to Kenya about 1,000 years

The camel is the most important livestock to the Gabbra tribe, which relies on the animal for its milk as their staple diet.

ago from what is today the Republic of the Sudan. The Masai are traditionally nomadic cattle herders and tend to be tall and slender with a reputation for being lion-hunters and fierce warriors. In spite of pressure to modernize, the Masai have maintained much of their traditional culture and way of life.

THE MAIN CUSHITIC PEOPLES

The Cushitic peoples make up only a small minority of Kenya's population, although they occupy a large area of the country. Scientists sometimes divide them into the Oromo, who come from Ethiopia, and the Somali. They occupy the north and northeast of Kenya, an extremely dry region that is often subject to drought and famine.

The main Oromo peoples include the Borana, Gabbra, Orma, and Rendille. The Rendille are nomads who make a living from herding camels. They live in the remote wilderness and as such have been less affected by outside contact than have the Masai. The Orma occupy the land on either side of the Tana River. The area is more fertile than its surroundings, so the Orma are able to keep herds of cattle and are famous for their long-horned Zebu-type cows.

The Somali are pastoralists who tend large herds of cattle, goats, sheep, and camels in the dry north of Kenya. They are among the people who have especially suffered from drought conditions in the country.

THE OUTSIDERS

Apart from the Africans, Kenya has small minority groups from other parts of the world. The first Arab traders came to Kenya nearly 1,000 years ago and so have long ties with the region. Most Kenyan Arabs live near the coast. With their bazaars and mosques, certain areas of Mombasa look as if they belong in the Middle East rather than Africa. Many Arabs are involved in trading, while others make a living fishing.

Kenya also has a large number of people who originate from the Indian subcontinent. They are generally referred to as Asians. At the turn of the century, thousands of Asians were brought to Kenya to work on the railway. Many stayed, often taking positions in the government or becoming traders. Today, the Asian community is still heavily involved in commerce and trading, although many work in professions such as accounting, medicine, engineering, and law.

A large number of Europeans fled Kenya when it became independent. Only Kenyans may own land, but all residents, whatever their color or background, are offered Kenyan citizenship. Some European Kenyans are prosperous farmers. However, most Caucasians living in Kenya are now expatriates working on short-term contracts.

SMALLER GROUPS IN KENYA

BANTU The Bantu group forms the largest group in Kenya's population. The smaller Bantu groups in Kenya include the Senguju, the Taita and Taveta, and the Tharaka.

The Taita and Taveta number around 300,000. They keep some animals and cultivate food such as millet, sweet potatoes, and tomatoes in the fertile Taita Hills in the southern part of Kenya. Many are Westernized and hold urban jobs. Most practice Christianity, although some of their traditional beliefs persist, such as seeking communion with the spirits of their ancestors for advice on important decisions.

The Tharaka number around 10,000. They form small villages and live in round-shaped homes with conical grass roofs on the low, hot plains of the Tana River Valley east of Mount Kenya. It is a harsh area, with endemic illnesses such as malaria and sleeping sickness. The Tharaka are famous for their witchcraft and colorful drums. They have preserved their centuries-old way of life, growing sorghum, green peas, millet, sunflowers, and cotton, and herding goats and cattle. They are also renowned beekeepers.

Samburu warriors are responsible for the safety of the tribe and cattle. Boys are taught to hunt from a young age.

CUSHITIC The smaller Cushitic groups in Kenya include the Boni and the El Molo. The Boni number around 4,000, in the coastal hinterland. They were originally hunter-gatherers and ivory traders. They depend entirely on nature for food and medicine. The main ingredient in the Boni's diet is honey. They track down honey by whistling to birds that guide them to the hives. The birds, known by locals as "Mirsi," are described as honey guides, and they feed on wax and bee larvae.

The El Molo make up the smallest ethnic group in Kenya and consist of only a few hundred people. They originally lived on two small islands in Lake Turkana. Fish form their basic diet, supplemented with crocodile meat. Some scientists think that the El Molo might be the descendents of the original inhabitants of Kenya.

NILOTIC The smaller Nilotic groups in Kenya include the Ilchamus, the Nandi, the Pokot, the Samburu, and the Turkana.

The Ilchamus, also known as Njemp, number around 40,000 along the shores of Lake Baringo. They are related to the Masai and speak Maa. The Ilchamus are mainly pastoralists, farmers, or fishermen. They are known especially for their exciting dances.

The Nandi take their name from their land in the beautiful Nandi Hills. They moved there between 300 and 400 years ago and learned to farm from their neighbors.

The Pokot number around 200,000 and live in the semiarid Great Rift Valley. Those living in the hills tend to be farmers, while those on the plains are usually cattle herders. The search for water and pasture often brings Pokot herders into contact with the Turkana, and cattle raids occur between the two groups.

The Samburu, numbering around 70,000 in Kenya, live in the highlands around Mount Nyiro and on the arid plain below. The Samburu are part of the Maa-speaking group and share many similarities with the Masai such as their physical appearance and style of dress. The Samburu are also traditionally cattle herders, though some have taken up farming, and they too take pride in their warriors.

The Turkana number around 300,000 and live along the shores of Lake Turkana. They are related to the Samburu and Masai and are also known for their fierce warriors. However, unlike the Masai, the Turkana have remained relatively untouched by modernization. The Turkana economy is centered on cattle and camels, but they also fish in Lake Turkana.

INTERNET LINKS

www.bluegecko.org/kenya/tribes/kikuyu/index.htm

This website has detailed information on the music and culture of Kenya with links to different pages, including a link to Kikuyu and other ethnic groups.

www.international.iupui.edu/kenya/resources/Lecture-Notes-for-a-History-of-Kenya.pdf

This is a link to a very informative pdf file entitled Lecture Notes on the History of Kenya by Prof. Anne Nangulu.

www.bluegecko.org/

This is the encyclopedic multimedia website of writer and traveler Jens Finke, with information on the traditional music and cultures of Kenya.

LIFESTYLE

Women sell rice at a busy market in Meru, where many Kenyans come to purchase daily necessities.

7

TRADITION IS DYING in Kenya. First the early missionaries and then the modern government have tried to introduce new ideas and change old customs. While their actions have benefitted the local people in some ways, such as reducing the influence of black magic, many healthy traditions have suffered at the hands of modernity.

THE ROLE OF THE FAMILY

Kenyan society has traditionally revolved around the family. The term family is often used very broadly and may include distant relations. In cities, the help and support shown to the family is often extended to anybody from the same village or group. Family bonds are strong. People who move to urban areas usually try to send money home to support their family members in the village.

Old people hold honored positions and are cared for and respected in Kenyan society. One impact of the acquired immunodeficiency syndrome (AIDS) epidemic has been that grandparents, who had counted on being looked after in their old age by their children, are finding that they may have to look after their orphaned grandchildren.

Traditionally, important decisions were always made at a gathering of the elders of the village. In modern Kenya, that power has passed to government-appointed officials.

Kenyans enjoy a reputation of being hard workers and it is quite normal for the streets to be crowded at 7.00 A.M. in the morning. Even so, Kenyans generally have a casual approach to time and are quite relaxed. The phrase "*Hakuna Matata*" can be translated from Swahili to mean "there are no worries," or "no problem."

BIRTH

In 1996 a Kenyan women's group promoted a new and safe coming-of-age rite for girls. In this ceremony, girls receive a week of counseling on how to cope with adolescence and womanhood. This is followed by a community celebration, but there is no operation.

Traditionally birth is considered a great occasion, and the mother-to-be is attended by several midwives. The Kikuyu believe that the placenta and umbilical cord symbolize the attachment of the child to the mother and its roots in the traditional society. The placenta is deposited in an uncultivated field and covered with grass and grains as a symbol of fertility. The Luo believe that the placenta of a girl must be buried on the left-hand side of her mother's house but the placenta of a boy must be buried on the right. This is because within the Luo symbolic and cosmological system, the left side relates to impermanency and vulnerability, while the right relates to authority and permanency. Girls are regarded as impermanent tribal members as they will move outside the family when married, but boys are regarded as authoritative and permanent as they will carry on as patriarchal authorities.

The birth is often followed by a period of seclusion. When the mother emerges from her home to show the new baby to her friends, a goat might be sacrificed and a feast held. The arrival of a new baby is seen as an event for the whole village to celebrate.

For the parents, a baby girl brings the promise of future wealth because daughters can bring a marriage dowry. Sons are believed to carry the spirits of the ancestors and form a link with the past. The prestige of the new parents also increases with the birth of a son. The father might gain a higher level of elderhood in his community.

In villages where medical assistance is scarce, many babies die at birth. The infant mortality rate in Kenya in 2011 was estimated to be 42 deaths for every 1,000 live births. The Kenyan government has tried to provide better care for women having babies. The amount of care a woman receives varies across economic groups and from region to region. Many Kenyan mothers give birth in the absence of medical professionals and depend on traditional midwives or family members to help them.

Some traditional midwives have considerable experience and are very good at their work. Recent projects have tried to extend these women's knowledge by offering them education and advice on matters such as modern hygiene. Traditional midwives have also been trained to help in the fight against AIDS and female circumcision.

PUBERTY

When children reach puberty, many groups will circumcise both boys and girls. This is a sign that the children have reached adulthood. Boys will usually go through the operation between the ages of 12 and 15. They will be expected to endure the operation without showing any sign of pain.

In middle-class families, the circumcision may be conducted by a modern doctor. In the villages and poor areas of the city, the operation is more likely to be performed by a village elder with experience but no medical training.

Three youths stand with their mentor, responsible for initiating them into tribe traditions. During this time—which includes a period of seclusion following their circumcision—they wear skins made of cow hide and carry staves.

In some ethnic groups, the periods before and after circumcision are times of seclusion. The young people are then considered to have left the village as children to return as adults. While they are away they might receive instructions from older people to prepare them for their new responsibilities as adults. The circumcision ceremony is particularly important to groups such as the Masai as it initiates the boys into the warrior stage of their lives. When they return to the village, they have their heads shaved and are recognized as men. They are then known as *moran* (MAH-ren) and live in isolated rough camps in the bush learning tribal customs and developing courage, strength, and endurance with other men of their age.

If conducted hygienically, male circumcision is not dangerous. In societies where daily hygiene might be a problem, it has medical advantages in reducing infectious diseases. On the other hand, female circumcision may range from minor to major operations, depending on the group, and may cause trauma or bleeding. Yet there are enormous cultural and familial pressures for girls to be circumcised. In some parts of Kenya, uncircumcised women may find difficulty finding a husband from the same community. A motion seeking to ban female circumcision was defeated in the Kenyan parliament in 1996. The Children's Act of 2001 protected children against this cultural practice but it is still carried out, especially among pastoral communities. The practice was finally declared illegal in 2011.

EDUCATION

Many Kenyans, especially in the cities, place considerable importance on education. Kenyan children have received free elementary education since the Kibaki government came to power. Kenya's education structure consists of 8 years of elementary school, 4 years of high school, and 4 years of college. The main subjects studied are mathematics, geography, and Kiswahili. English is the medium of instruction. There are exams for entering high school and college, and competition for placement is tough.

Visitors from the Western nations might find that many Kenyan schools have very little equipment. In addition, the low pay makes it difficult to find qualified teachers. In the city slums or remote rural areas, the teachers are young men and women who have only a high-school education. Despite these problems the education program succeeded in raising literacy rates to 85.1 percent. Fewer women than men are literate because the women have less access to education and are expected to help with gathering firewood, collecting water, and cultivating farms.

Kindergarten children have a computer lesson in their school at Wema Centre, a non-governmental organization that offers rehabilitation programmes for street children.

The revised Education Bill of 2012 states that every child has the right to free and compulsory basic education. It is compulsory for every child who is born in Kenya or resides in Kenya to attend school regularly. The same Bill also states that a child of compulsory school age may not be employed in any labor or occupation that prevents the child from attending school. People in some of the more traditional groups, such as the Masai, have mixed feelings about education. While seeing the benefits, many also believe that the education offered by the government does not consider their own traditions and values.

HEALTH

Health care has improved considerably since independence. There are good hospitals in the cities, although the best are private and expensive. There are clinics in most villages, and progress has been made in providing clean water and educating Kenyans to take better care of their health.

The average life expectancy in Kenya is 63 years of age. This is below the U.S. or European standards. This low life expectancy is largely a result of the AIDS epidemic. In 2011 it was estimated that approximately 1.5 million people were living with AIDS, or 6.3 percent of the population. Malaria is a great danger in many regions, and worm infestations and bilharziasis are common. Diseases such as leprosy and sleeping sickness persist, while obesity and heart disease are becoming more common as increasing affluence has made urban lifestyle and diet less healthy.

One of the largest concerns facing Kenya is infant mortality. According to the United Nations Children's Fund, in 2010 there were 128 deaths for every 1,000 children under five years of age. This figure is double the world average of 65 deaths per 1,000 children. Most children's health initiatives target diseases, such as AIDS, malaria, and measles. But pneumonia is the cause of more deaths in children under the age of 5 in Kenya than all three diseases combined. In 2011 a new vaccine to combat pneumococcus which can trigger pneumonia and meningitis was made available, free of charge, to children under a year old. Kenya was the first country to publicly administer the vaccine that was part of an initiative funded by the Global Alliance for Vaccines and Immunization.

A simple medical clinic. Many factors inhibit Kenyans from receiving proper healthcare, such as improper utilization of resources and underfinancing of the health sector.

MARRIAGE

Most Kenyan cultures demand a dowry that is paid by the husband's family to the family of the bride. Traditionally, it would be paid in cattle or other livestock. Today, especially among urban families, the dowry may be in cash or electrical goods. The payment of the dowry may be made shortly before the marriage or over many years, from the time of birth to years after the marriage. The dowry system means that some marriages are arranged by the families, and the young people's feelings toward each other are not always taken into account.

In a traditional wedding, a feast will be arranged at the husband's house, after which the couple are recognized as married. Today many Kenyans opt for Christian church weddings similar to those celebrated in the West. It is considered important to put on a show for everybody, and many families borrow money and go into debt to pay for a big wedding.

It is still common for Kenyan men to marry more than one wife. It is a man's duty to provide a separate home for each wife, often miles apart. In such marriages there is a hierarchy among the wives, with the senior wife usually enjoying more authority and influence.

In many ways polygamy is intended as an insurance policy. Each wife looks after a proportion of her husband's animals, so that if there is an outbreak of disease, the family might not lose all its herds. Education and exposure to Western cultures has made many women question the practice of polygamy and arranged marriages.

In 2011, proposals in the new Marriage Bill sought to introduce changes in the institution of marriage. Payment of a dowry would become optional while polygamy would be legalized. The proposed bill stated that marriage shall be between a man and a woman. A couple wishing to get married must give the Registrar 21 days notice and indicate whether it will be a monogamous or potentially polygamous marriage. If the intended husband is already married, the names of existing wives must be indicated in the notice. The marriage may be contracted in civil form, under customary law, Islamic form, Hindu ceremonies, or Christian rites.

THE ROLE OF WOMEN IN KENYA

Kenya, like most African nations, is a male-dominated society. Women constitute over 50 percent of Kenya's population but the literacy rate is lower than that of the men, and they also tend to be poorer. It has been suggested that African women do 80 percent of the work but receive almost none of the money. In the village a woman's work may include helping on the farm, selling surplus crops in the market, and fetching and carrying water and goods. Many homes are without a convenient water supply, so thousands of women have to carry heavy containers of water home from the nearest well.

Very few Kenyan women own land, and relatively few can find good jobs. For many women the only hope of a better life is to find a husband. Yet violence and sexual abuse against women are widespread, and such occurrences within a family are often ignored.

If her husband dies, a woman might face serious problems because women rarely inherit property. This means she might be thrown out of her house or forced to leave the land she has farmed for years. There are proposals to amend Kenyan laws to protect women in this situation, while Kenya's customary laws tend to favor men.

This attitude toward women affects all levels of society. Women are poorly represented in the Kenyan parliament. Nevertheless, a growing number of Kenyan women have become excellent role models to inspire change. These women include the conservationist Wangari Maathai and Lornah Kiplagat, one of Kenya's best runners. Maathai came to world attention in 1998 when she fought against a housing project that threatened the Karura Forest. In 2003 she became the deputy minister in the Ministry of Environment, Resources, and Wildlife, and in 2004 she was awarded the Nobel Peace Prize. Kiplagat won the Los Angeles Marathon twice and set up the first high-altitude training camp in Kenya that caters to professional and nonprofessional runners from all over the world who can train there the whole year round in perfect conditions. She qualified for the Olympic Games held in London in 2012.

A group of women work on a farm, cultivating the land. Women workers earn less than men despite carrying out the same job, which shows the ongoing prevalence of gender inequality in the country.

IN THE VILLAGE

Life in a typical village revolves around the crops. Generally, people go to bed early and wake up at sunrise. After working in the fields, the men spend the evening talking and exchanging stories. Occasionally, the whole family makes a trip to town to buy items such as blankets, lamps, and tools.

People who depend on livestock have a different lifestyle than those who farm. The areas they live in tend to be drier, meaning people move around to find food and water for their animals. Old people, women, and young children might live in a permanent or semipermanent village at the center of the animal range.

More and more Kenyans are leaving the countryside to seek work in the cities. They find that working the land for a living is difficult and barely brings in enough to feed themselves and their families. Even contented farmers or livestock keepers might be forced to leave during times of drought. Traditionally, farmers divide the land among their sons, but a point comes where the plots are too small and not all the sons can inherit land. That forces many young men to leave the village to find work. Young people, especially educated ones, are also not content to live the same lives their parents do.

IN THE CITY

For rich Kenyans, city life offers a standard of living similar to that in the West. It is considered important in urban society to demonstrate one's status and wealth. Rich Kenyans drive expensive cars as a status symbol.

Life is harder for middle-class people. They might earn more money than Kenyans living in the countryside, but living in the city is also more expensive. Over the last few years the cost of living has risen faster than wages, and a long recession has meant that many people have lost their jobs.

The cities suffer from problems such as crime, pollution, and congestion. Nairobi and Mombasa do not have good electricity and telephone services, and bribes are necessary before any repair work is done. Still, Nairobi offers better work opportunities and a higher quality of education. The city also has an exciting entertainment scene.

Informal settlements form a significant part of city life and are home to 60 percent of the urban population. There are approximately 2.5 million people living in about 200 settlements. Yet the big settlements occupy only 6 percent of the land. One such settlement is Kibera, the largest in Africa and home to approximately 500,000 to 700,000 people. Life is hard here and the residents only find occasional work in the city. Others might have their own businesses in Kibera, such as bringing in water to sell, renting out rooms, or opening little bars. The average size of a shack in Kibera is 12 feet by 12 feet. It is built with mud walls, a corrugated tin roof, and a dirt or concrete floor. As many as eight people may live in one shack, often sleeping on the floor. Until recently Kibera had no water and it had to be collected from the Nairobi Dam. Outbreaks of cholera and typhoid were common. Now there are two mains water pipes into Kibera. One is from the municipal council and one from the World Bank. Residents collect and pay for clean water. Sanitary hygiene is low, and in most of Kibera there are no toilet facilities. One latrine is shared by up to 50 shacks. Only about 20 percent of Kibera has electricity. UN-Habitat is working with the government of Kenya to improve accessibility to water and sanitation. Improvements are to be made to the drainage system. Door-to-door waste collection and recycling initiatives are being introduced. The project is also trying to establish the Kibera Bicycle Transport Project (KBTP) by engaging local artisans in the design and manufacture of bicycle/tricycle trailer systems for multipurpose use by the local community.

One of the saddest sights in modern Kenya is of street children. They have a hard life and earn a living by guarding cars or begging for money. Many turn to crime or prostitution to survive.

INTERNET LINKS

www.education.go.ke/Home.aspx?department=1

Official website of the Ministry of Education in Kenya.

www.lornah.com/

Official website of the High Altitude Training Centre in Iten, Kenya, founded by Lornah Kiplagat.

www.kibera.org.uk/default.html

This is the official website of Kibera UK, a charity that helps volunteers work in Kibera. The website has information on Kibera, the largest informal settlement in Nairobi.

RELIGION

Baluchi Mosque in Mombasa Old Town. The mosque was expertly made from wood and possesses a clean and sophisticated structure.

8

PEOPLE IN KENYA are free to worship in any way they wish. Many Kenyans have converted to Christianity and a smaller number to Islam. Christianity was introduced to Kenya in 1846 by European missionaries, while Islam arrived with Arab settlers in A.D. 700.

However, traditional African religions have survived in many communities, practiced in their complete form or partially incorporated into the practice of other faiths.

It is believed that a proportion of Kenyans still follow traditional religions, though it is impossible to obtain an accurate figure. People may not readily admit that they practice a traditional religion. In addition, many people combine some of their old beliefs with those of another religion.

Traditional African religions existed in Kenya before the arrival of Islam and Christianity. Although different from group to group, most of these religions share some common points, such as the belief that every natural object possesses a soul or spirit.

THE SUPREME BEING

All the traditional religions believe in a single great being that was the creator of the world and that provided the people with everything they needed to live. This creator, portrayed as being masculine, is known by different names often within the same ethnic group.

Mulungu is the name given to the supreme being by many Kenyans, including the Kamba and Meru. That name is also used by people in other parts of East Africa, some living as far away as the northern border of Zimbabwe. The Kikuyu call their creator Ngai, a name they probably borrowed from the Masai people, while the Luhya call their supreme being Were, the god of Mount Elgon.

The supreme being can never be seen directly but manifests himself in the sun, moon, and stars. He might visit the earth to reward or punish people. On these visits he is said to rest on the great mountains, and thunder and lightning are believed to be signs that he is moving across the sky.

THE STORY OF CREATION

Different groups have their own stories to describe how the earth was created, and there are often variations of the story within a group. The Kikuyu, for example, believe that Ngai chose a man named Gikuyu to be the father of the Kikuyu and gave him Mumbi as his wife. Gikuyu was taken to a high mountain and shown all the land below. He was told to go forth and populate the land. Gikuyu and Mumbi produced nine daughters but no sons. So the couple returned to Ngai, who created nine husbands for their daughters. The nine couples founded the nine clans of the Kikuyu.

The Masai also call the creator of the world Ngai. They believe that he appears as a red cloud when angry and as a black cloud when pleased. They believe that Ngai lives in the sky above Mount Kilimanjaro and that he gave them cattle to sustain them. That is why the Masai raid other people's cattle herds—to reclaim what they believe is already theirs.

SPIRITS

Traditional African beliefs include the existence of spirits and their influence on people. It is considered important to make the spirits happy or else they might bring illness or bad luck. Although beliefs vary, the important spirits can generally be broken into two groups: the spirits of family members who have died, of whom a person's parents are the most important, and other spirits.

A veterinarian who had trained in Nairobi went into a village where a man's cattle were dying. He explained the cattle had a disease that could be cured with medicine and that this was not magic or the work of spirits.

The man happily accepted the medicine for his cattle but asked if the veterinarian could explain why the disease had struck his animals, but not those of his neighbors?

The veterinarian admitted he could not.

"That is what I must go to the witch doctor to find out," said the farmer.

The spirits of deceased family members look after the living family members and are believed to exist alongside the living, in a realm that is somewhere between the world of god and the world of humans. This means that spirits can act as intermediaries between people and god.

There are good and bad spirits, and gifts are offered to the bad spirits to keep them from mischief. Gifts acknowledge the presence of the spirits but are not offered in worship.

Other spirits are believed to dwell in deserted places, such as the forest or a particularly dry area. However, they sometimes approach human settlements or reveal themselves to people who wander too close to them.

Communicating with spirits Kenyans developed a culture of divination to contact spirits and try to influence them. There are also medicine men and traditional healers. The role of each can vary between ethnic groups and between villages. Some diviners claim to have special abilities.

Diviners are believed to be able to look into the spirit world. Somebody experiencing a run of bad luck can ask a diviner to locate the spirits causing the problem and suggest a magical cure. Some diviners can also use the spirits to see into the future. In his book, *Facing Mount Kenya*, Jomo Kenyatta relates the story of a wise Kikuyu man who saw in a vision the coming of the Europeans with their guns and railroads. The Masai have their own fortune-tellers and medicine men, whom they call *laibon* (LAI-bon). One method they use for fortune-telling is to read the message in pebbles cast from a gourd. The services of a *laibon* may be engaged to settle family disputes or predict the success of a cattle raid.

During the 19th century, there was a powerful movement in Europe to convert the world to Christianity. Africa became a favorite destination for enthusiastic young missionaries. It was believed that commerce, civilization, and Christianity should be used to educate the Africans and bring them into the mainstream of world events.

The first missionaries arrived in Kenya in the early 1840s and slowly spread inland to the Great Rift Valley. They offered training in farming, handicraft making, and health care. Because it was necessary to read the Bible to understand Christianity, the church also established the first schools. Johann Ludwig Krapf (1810—81), a missionary who was also the first European to see Mount Kenya, translated the Bible into Kiswahili so that the Holy Book could be easily understood by Kenyans.

Many Kenyans were genuinely interested in the Christian faith, and the Kenyan church grew strong. However, although the early missionaries did a lot to improve the welfare of people in Kenya, critics have commented that they were insensitive to local traditions and culture. Claims have also been made that the missionaries might have done more to protect the local people from exploitation by the colonialists.

There are also medicine men or women who have detailed knowledge of traditional medicines. Some of the potions they offer make use of healing herbs, but much of their craft is based on magic.

In addition, there are witches and sorcerers. They have abilities that are similar to the diviners but misuse the power to cause harm to others. Traditional healers are engaged to detect witches and to heal a cursed person.

SACRIFICES

Many Kenyan families who still believe in the old traditional ways will set a little food and drink aside as offerings to the spirits of their ancestors.

Many tribes, including the Kikuyu, will also make a sacrifice during the important times in the farming cycle, such as planting or harvesting, and before major events such as weddings and circumcisions. Sacrifices might also be made at times of epidemic or drought.

Several years of Jesus' life are unaccounted for and the English have a song "Jerusalem" which suggests Jesus might have visited Great Britain during this spell.

The people of Mbale, in Vihiga District, also believe that Jesus might have visited them, perhaps during his 40 days in the wilderness. This belief is based on some strange marks that appear to be large human footprints pressed into the rocks. Some people even claim that scratches on these rocks are actually Hebrew writing.

Goats or sheep are the usual animals that are sacrificed. There is no record of human sacrifice in Kenyan society, although it might have happened in the distant past, for there are several legends and fables about human sacrifice.

THE DARK SIDE

Many Kenyan people still believe that witchcraft can be used to cause illness, bad luck or even death. Witches, or sorcerers, are people born with the magical power of diviners, but who misuse that power against their neighbors. Witch doctors are employed to detect witches. They might also offer cures and protection to a person who has had a curse placed on them.

Sadly each year there are stories of people in villages being murdered by mobs, who believe they have been dealing in witchcraft.

RELIGIOUS PLACES

There are no churches or temples for those following an animistic religion, but there might be places that have a religious significance. This is likely to be some quiet secluded spot, often under an old tree, where people can go to reflect.

Mountains are generally considered holy places to the tribes living close to them. The mountaintops are often covered in clouds, which make them more mysterious, and they are linked with the arrival of the vital rains.

The people living on the lower slopes of Mount Kenya used to climb the mountain to make their offerings. They would also construct their houses so that the main entrance faced the mountain, and bury their dead with their heads toward the mountain.

CHRISTIANITY

The majority of Kenyans are Christians. Christianity was brought to Africa by European missionaries. The African people had little problem assimilating their own belief in a supreme being with the Christian concept of god. However, Christianity had many conflicts with traditional practices, particularly polygamy. In most Kenyan societies, men were encouraged to marry more than one wife. This was seen as a sign of wealth and brought prestige within the community.

Despite such differences, Christianity has had considerable success in gaining converts among agricultural people such as the Kikuyu. By contrast, the cattle-herding groups such as the Masai have largely resisted the faith.

The Kenyan church has long been involved in politics. At first the church helped the colonial authorities control the African population. But during the 1950s an increasing number of African pastors supported the call for independence in their sermons. The church was also one of the strongest voices in opposing President Moi and calling for the return of democracy to Kenya.

The traditional denominations in Kenya are often seen as a legacy of European rule, and many Kenyan Christians have broken away to set up their own churches. The newer churches are often more sympathetic to indigenous beliefs or customs.

The largest independent church is the Church of Christ in Africa, with its cathedral in Nairobi. It aims much of its teaching at the urban poor and offers traditional education and healing to the poor and needy.

ISLAM

About 10 percent of Kenya's population is Muslim. While most Muslims live on the coast, many have migrated to the cities, where large mosques have been built. There are also Muslims among the Somali-speaking people in the eastern provinces and among the Asian community. After the 1998 bombing of the U.S. embassy in Nairobi, the government temporarily closed a number of Islamic charity organizations, believing that they were being used to support terrorists.

A Catholic church built by Italian prisoners of war in the 1940s is situated on the slopes of the Rift Valley. The British and Italians were of different faiths, therefore the former allocated the latter a small piece of land for a place of worship.

Colorful stones were hand carved by skilled sculptors over a span of two years and exhibited in the Shri Swaminarayan Mandir temple in Nairobi.

INDIAN RELIGIONS

Most Asians in Kenya are Hindus and have their own temples. Hinduism has had little impact on the African population, and there has been no attempt to convert people. There are other small groups, such as the Sikhs and the Jains.

INTERNET LINKS

www.minorityrights.org/3/home/mrg-directory-homepage.html

This website has information on the world's minorities and indigenous peoples.

www.africaimagelibrary.com/

The Africa Image Library website has images of Kenyan lifestyle and culture, including religion and traditional medicine men.

www.everyculture.com/

This website contains information on the culture of Kenya, including religion, diviners, medicine, rituals, and holy places.

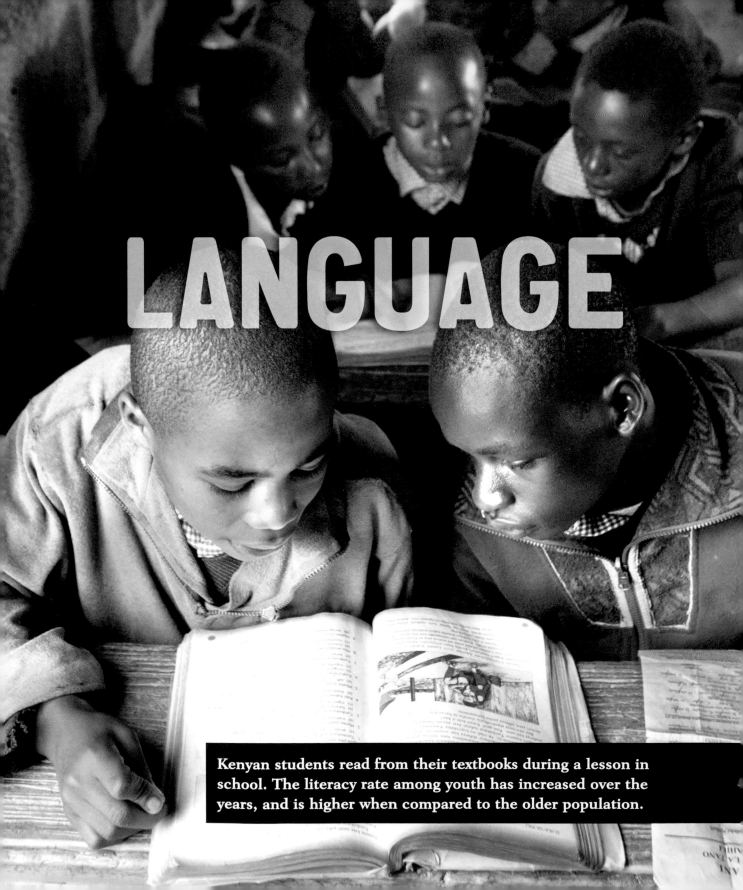

LANGUAGE

Kenyan students read from their textbooks during a lesson in school. The literacy rate among youth has increased over the years, and is higher when compared to the older population.

9

KISWAHILI AND ENGLISH are the official languages of Kenya. They serve as the common platform of communication in a country where many different ethnic languages are spoken.

Kiswahili was originally spoken only on the coast, but Arab traders and European missionaries spread its use into the interior. The colonial authorities and then the independent government encouraged Kenyans to learn Kiswahili as a means of communicating across ethnic groups.

It is not unusual for Kenyans to speak at least three languages: a mother tongue at home, Kiswahili in the city, and English at work. Those

Kenya is a multilingual country with two official languages: English and Kiswahili. The former was inherited from colonial rule when Kenya was part of the British Empire from 1920 to 1963. Kenya's urban population speak English, Kiswahili, and their mother tongue. Rural and peri-urban populations are less multilingual. In the very remote villages people may speak only their native language.

A mixture of English and Swahili books at a stationary stall in Nakuru.

Kiswahili is spoken over a large part of East Africa and in South Africa, and it has become increasingly recognized as an international language. Radio stations such as Voice of America and the British Broadcasting Corporation have broadcasted and maintain websites in Kiswahili. Michael Jackson used some Kiswahili words in his song Liberian Girl, *and moviegoers around the world heard the expression* hakuna matata *(hah-KOO-nah mah-TAH-tah), or no problems, in the movie* The Lion King.

living in the countryside might also speak the language of their neighbors. Yet, at the same time, one might also find some older men and many women in the villages who only speak their own languages.

KISWAHILI

Besides being an official language in Kenya, Tanzania, Zanzibar, and Uganda, Kiswahili is spoken in the big cities and commercial centers of Burundi and Rwanda and is understood in Uganda, northern Mozambique, northern Zambia, and southern Ethiopia. A dialect of Kiswahili called Kingwana is spoken in the Democratic Republic of the Congo.

There are about 80 million Africans who speak Kiswahili, although only an estimated 2 million use it as their first language. Kiswahili has 15 major dialects. In 1930 a committee representing Kenya, Tanzania, Uganda, and Zanzibar decided that Kiunguja, a coastal dialect used in Zanzibar, should become the official standard Kiswahili. The standard is used for radio broadcasts and in schools. There are two other important dialects: Kimvita and Kiamu. Kimvita is spoken in Mombasa, while Kiamu is used on Lamu Island and in the coastal areas close to it. People coming from Zanzibar, Pemba, and Lamu would understand each other, but they would be aware that the person they are speaking comes from a different region.

Kiswahili has been adapted in some unusual ways. The white people who came to Kenya in the colonial days often spoke a very simple form of Swahili, which became known as "pidgin Swahili."

Although many people call the language as Swahili, it is not technically correct. The ki- *prefix is a language marker. The English language is therefore* Kiingereza *and French is* Kifaransa. *The language of the Kamba tribe is Kikamba, and the language of the Swahili people is Kiswahili.*

The u- *prefix is a region or country marker, hence Germany is* Ujerumani *and Japan is* Ujapani. *Also, the prefix* m- *denotes speaker, while* wa- *indicates speakers. Examples are* Mfaransa, *or French speaker, and* Wajerumani, *or German speakers.*

More recently young people in Nairobi have developed Sheng. The name Sheng was derived from the first and middle letters of the word Swahili and the first three letters of the word English. This is a street language, probably inspired by the speech of Afro-Americans, which young Kenyans have seen on TV and in movies. Sheng uses the grammar and syntax of Kiswahili, but mixes Swahili and English words (and sometimes words from a tribal language) to produce a distinctive "language." Parents listening to their children speaking Sheng would probably not understand what they are saying, even though they would understand most of the words!

Sheng is changing all the time, and can vary from one small group of friends to another. The only really important rule is to sound "cool." The language was once associated with thugs, *matatu* drivers and Nairobi's youth. Once described as the language of bus conductors and football teams it has been taken up by and become fashionable with many young middle-class Kenyans. Sheng was once a highly stigmatized language but is gaining legitimacy and greater presence in Kenya's multilingual environment. It is now used in print, on television and radio, music, and political slogans.

A CHANGING LANGUAGE Over the years, Kiswahili has borrowed many words from other languages, particularly Arabic. The early Arabs brought many things to Africa that the Africans had not seen before, so the Africans adopted the Arabic words to describe them. Examples include *kahawa*, or coffee; *kitabu*, or book; and *biashara*, or business. The word Swahili is itself an Arabic word that means "coastal people."

1	— moja	11	— kumi na moja *(10 and 1)*
2	— mbili	13	— kumi na tatu *(10 and 3)*
3	— tatu	20	— ishirini
4	— nne	100	— mia
5	— tano	101	— mia na moja *(100 and 1)*
6	— sita	110	— mia moja na kumi *(100 and 10)*
7	— saba		
8	— nane		
9	— tisa		
10	— kumi		

An animal vocabulary chart in English, Kiswahili, and the local vernacular in Kenya.

With the arrival of the Europeans, more new words were needed, and there were often adaptations of the English words. For example, the Kiswahili word for bicycle is *baisikeli*, motor car is *motokaa*, ticket is *tiketi*, and blanket is *blanketi*. More recent additions include words such as *kompyuta*, or computer. Portuguese and German words can also be found in the language, such as *leso*, adapted from a Portuguese word that means handkerchief, and *shule*, German for school. The borrowing of words has not been a one-way process. Kiswahili has given the world such words as impala and safari, both now established in the English language.

WRITING IT DOWN Kiswahili was one of the first written African languages. The early Arab settlers used their own script to write chronicles in Kiswahili. Today, Kiswahili is usually written using the Latin alphabet.

The early missionaries developed grammar and spelling rules for recording Kiswahili, based on the rules of the English language. Their work formed the basis of today's accepted style, which is known as the East African Standard. The style is used in Kenya, Uganda, and Tanzania.

PROBLEMS WITH KISWAHILI Kiswahili is often spoken badly. It has a reputation for being an easy language to learn but a difficult language to speak well. Although President Kenyatta made Kiswahili the official parliamentary language of the National Assembly in 1974, speeches and written government reports could only be made in English.

With the promulgation of the new constitution in 2012 Kiswahili and English are both official languages. Kiswahili is compulsory and examinable in schools. Kiswahili can now be used in official documents. However, by law the only language recognized for proceedings in the High Court and in the Court of Appeal is English. Although many radio stations broadcast in Kiswahili, only one daily newspaper is published in the language.

Kenya has about 10 newspapers published in English. *The Daily Nation* is the most distinguished paper, with a daily circulation of more than 200,000.

WORDS AND EXPRESSIONS

Probably the first word any visitor hears in Kiswahili is *jambo* (JAM-boh), meaning hello. When speaking to a man, it is polite to address him as *bwana* (BWAH-nah), a contraction of *baba wa wana*, meaning the father of many sons. On entering a house, one will likely be greeted with *kari-bu* (kar-i-BOO), which means welcome. *Asante* (ah-SAN-tay) means thank you and is often used with *sana* to mean thank you very much. The word *harambee*, or pull

NATIONAL, OFFICIAL, AND OTHER LANGUAGES

The new constitution of Kenya, 2010, states that the national language of the Republic is Kiswahili. The official languages of the Republic are Kiswahili and English. It also states that the diversity of language of the people of Kenya will be promoted and protected, and that the development and use of indigenous languages, Kenyan Sign language, Braille, and other communication formats and technologies accessible to persons with disabilities will be promoted.

together, has a national significance in Kenyan culture, as does *uhuru* (oo-HOO-roo), which means freedom, liberty, or independence.

Sentences and expressions are often built around a root word. For example, *penda* is the root word for like. *Kupenda* means to like. If one wants to say "I like," it would be *ninapenda*. *Ninakupenda* means I like you and translates word for word as I-you-like.

People in Kenya tell the time differently from the way people do in Western countries. The new day starts when the sun rises at 6 A.M., not at the stroke of midnight. What the 24-hour system marks as 7 AM is in Swahili time 1 o'clock in the morning, or the end of the first hour of the morning.

INDIGENOUS LANGUAGES

There are a large number of languages spoken in Kenya by the various ethnic groups. Some of them, such as Gikuyu, Luo, and Luhya, are spoken by millions of Kenyans.

Writer Ngugi wa Thiong'o was the first East African to write a major novel in English. He later switched to writing in Kenyan languages. That made his work accessible to a wider audience in Kenya and helped to halt the decline in ethnic languages.

According to a report by the UNESCO in 2012, nearly 3,000 languages spoken around the world today are endangered and will disappear by the end of this century. Of these languages 13 are in Kenya. A language usually becomes endangered when members of a small community find themselves outnumbered by their neighbors. They start using their neighbors' languages in everyday dealings. Within a couple of generations the language is lost among the young, leaving only a few elders who know their mother tongue.

KENYAN NAMES

During colonial times, Africans who were baptized were required to take European names. President Kenyatta himself used the name Johnstone Kamau when he attended missionary school. On entering politics, he reverted to his African name, Jomo Kenyatta. European names such as David, William, and Susan are common in Kenya. Some English surnames, such as Benson or Wilson, are also widely used in Kenya as Christian names. In addition, English names that have gone out of fashion in the rest of the world remain popular in Kenya. Julius, Wilfred, and Ernest are examples. Biblical names, such as Moses or Noah, are also widely used. However, an increasing number of Kenyans are choosing African names. Traditional African names include Odhiambo and Jomo.

Islamic names are very popular among Kenya's Muslim population. It is not unusual to find Kenyans with names such as Ibrahim, Salim, Muhammad, or Aisha.

INTERNET LINKS

www.mwanasimba.online.fr/E_index.html

The Mwana Simba website contains a new Kiswahili learning method for beginner students and has links to areas of study, such as verbs, conjugation tables, proverbs, and songs.

www.ethnologue.com/

An online encyclopedic reference work cataloging all the world's languages. Browse the country index to find the entry for Kenya.

www.magicalkenya.com/

Website with information on Kenya, including many images and links.

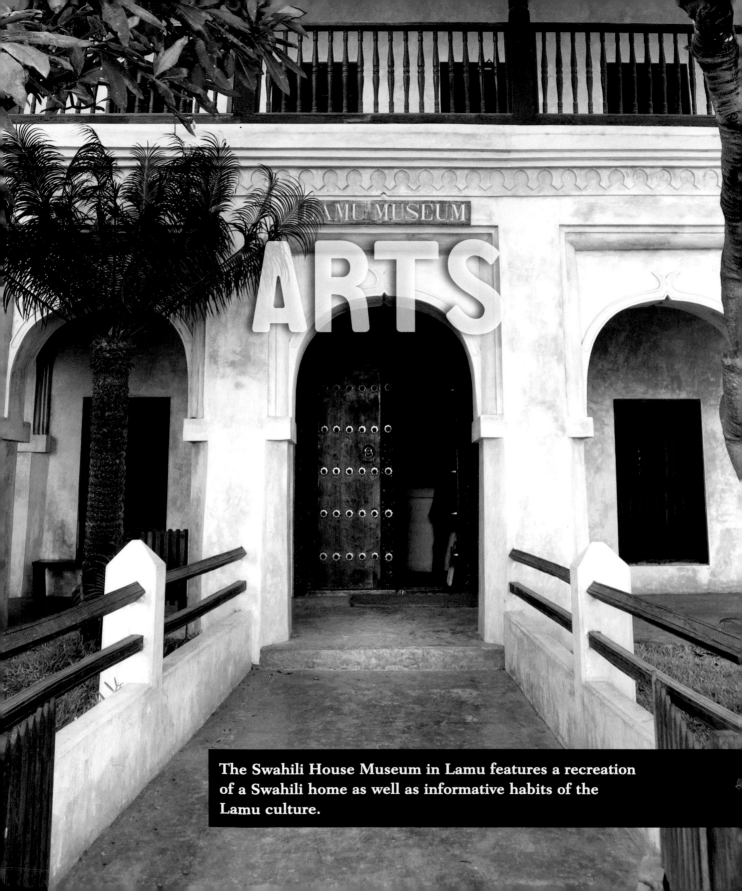

ARTS

The Swahili House Museum in Lamu features a recreation of a Swahili home as well as informative habits of the Lamu culture.

10

MUSIC AND DANCE are the most important forms of artistic expression in traditional Kenyan society. Both have a religious significance and are often used as a means to contact the spirit world. Storytelling is also important, although before the arrival of the Arabs and Europeans, there was no way to record Kenyan tales.

Today more Kenyans are becoming aware of the importance of their cultural heritage. At the same time the country is increasingly influenced by the Western music, literature, and art. It was once feared that Kenyan artists would just copy Western styles. However, today there is more confidence that talented Kenyans will take Western artistic ideas and fuse them with Kenyan art forms to produce new and vibrant works.

TRADITIONAL MUSIC AND DANCE

In Kenya, each ethnic group has its own music that has been used in centuries-old rituals. Traditionally, African music's most important role was to accompany dances. Such music relied heavily on rhythm that could be produced by hitting sticks, stamping feet, clapping, or beating on a drum.

Most dances originally had some spiritual meaning. There were fertility dances, rainmaking dances, and dances to ask the spirits to grant a good harvest. Today, some dance troupes retain traditional Kenyan dance styles. Others have adapted modern dance ideas, costumes, and instruments—signs that Kenyan dance is alive and evolving.

Kenya enjoys a diverse mix of cultures and traditions. The art and culture of Kenya is unique and is represented through its traditions, customs, music, dance, handicrafts, jewelry, clothes, and paintings. The themes in Kenyan art represent the daily life of the people, with the main two cultures being that of the Swahili people and of the Masai people. Kenya is also known for its traditional tribal masks, baskets, and mats.

MUSICAL INSTRUMENTS Much of traditional Kenyan music is polyrhythmic, which means that different rhythms are played on different instruments concurrently.

The key instrument is a large drum called *ngoma* (n-GO-mah). It is made from a hollowed-out section of a tree trunk and an animal skin stretched over the top. Zebra skin is traditionally considered to make the best drum membranes. The word *ngoma* is still used to describe most forms of traditional music and dance.

Different drums are used throughout the country. The *sikuti* (si-KOO-ti) is a dance style of the Luhya of western Kenya. This energetic dance takes its name from the local name for the drum that accompanies the dance along with bells, long horns, and whistles.

Apart from the single-string bow, which probably developed from the hunting bow, there are African lyres that have more than 10 strings. They are often used to accompany singing in festivals and magical rites. One of the largest African lyres is the *obukano* (o-boo-KAHN-o), which has been described as the double bass of Africa. The *nyatiti* (ni-YAT-eet-ti) is a basic stringed instrument similar to a medieval lyre. It has a gentle sound and is usually played solo with a single singer, sometimes accompanied by bells. Ayub Ogada has become internationally famous as a modern master *nyatiti* player whose first album *En Maana Kuoyo* is a good introduction to the sound of the *nyatti*.

A unique music style called the *taarab* (TAA-rab) developed on the coast combining elements of African percussion with Arabic rhythms. Traditional *taarab* music involves a large group of musicians playing the traditional Arab *oud* combined with other stringed instruments and several vocalists.

The *mbira* (m-BIR-ah) is a box with narrow metal bands fixed at one end, each strip of metal tuned to a different pitch. To produce a tune these bands are twanged, usually with the thumb. The *mbira* is found all over Africa and is known by several names, including *sansa* (SAHN-sah) and *kalimba* (kah-

A Masai tribesman blows into a kudu horn, which produces a deep, guttural sound, during a dance ceremony.

LEEM-bah). Sometimes the *mbira* is referred to as a thumb piano or finger xylophone.

Ornately decorated large horns may accompany a dance or story. Flutes made from bamboo or some other hollow plant are another traditional wind instrument. They usually accompany stories rather than dances.

STORYTELLING

Storytellers can still make a living by traveling from village to village entertaining people with their folk tales. A story might last for hours. To hold the audience's attention, the storyteller needs humor and stage presence and must be able to adapt the stories according to the audience and the occasion. Storytelling is often accompanied by percussion music and performed with songs and dances. Storytelling sessions are interactive and involves the audience's participation.

Drum musicians at the Maulidi Festival in Lamu.

Many of Kenya's folk tales have animals as the main characters. The hare is a favorite hero of Kikuyu stories. It outwits lions and hyenas. The tortoise is another hero. Kenyan folk tales usually have a strong moral line, with the villains coming to some dreadful end.

Poetry might also be used to entertain people and can be recited or sung. The coastal Swahili people are particularly noted for their poetry, probably a result of Arab influence.

MODERN LITERATURE

The first Kenyan writers tended to produce autobiographies that described village life. Kenyatta's *Facing Mount Kenya* was one of the first such books. Since the 1950s, autobiographical accounts tended to concentrate on the independence struggle and the Mau Mau uprising. Most of the earlier writers were Kikuyu, although Grace Ogot (1930—) wrote some excellent accounts of life in a Luo community and was the first woman to have fiction published by the East African Publishing House. Her novel *The Promised Land* (1966) tells of Luo pioneers in Kenya and Tanzania.

The best-known Kenyan writer and the first to write novels is Ngugi wa Thiong'o (1938—). As a boy, Thiong'o was inspired by the storytellers who visited his village. They were a major influence on his writing career. His first novel, *Weep Not, Child*, was published in 1964. It was the first major novel published in English by an East African. It told of the conflict within a Kikuyu family divided by the Mau Mau rebellion. His best-known book, *Petals of Blood*, was published in 1977. It contrasts the life of the poor villagers with that of the newly rich and often corrupt Kenyans. During the 1970s other young writers started to emerge, such as Meja Mwangi (1948—), who wrote *Taste of Death* (1975), and Charles Mangua (1939—), whose books *Son of Woman* (1971) and *A Tail in the Mouth* (1972) were very popular. He was awarded the Jomo Kanyatta Prize for Literature for *A Tail in the Mouth*.

Kenyan literature went through a dormant stage in the 1980s and 1990s, partly the result of government interference. Ngugi himself was put in jail for his work, and publishers were wary of releasing books that could be seen as criticizing the government. Financial problems were also a major hindrance. There has always been a limited market for Kenyan literature, and local writers have found it almost impossible to make a living from their works.

Recent years have seen the first signs of a new generation of writers emerging. In 2002 Binyavanga Wainaina (1971—) won the prestigious Caine Prize for African Writing. *Discovering Home* describes Wainaina's return to Kenya after living in South Africa for 10 years.

THEATER

Although Kenya had many traditional storytellers who were talented performers, the concept of acting out a story was introduced to Kenya by the Europeans. There was a growth in African drama groups after independence. Ngugi wa Thiong'o led the way with plays such as *The Black Hermit* (1968). There was also an attempt to form traveling theaters to take plays out into the countryside. The Kamiriithu Theater became a center for political drama and protest about social conditions.

For many years Kenyan theater was suppressed by the government. Since the 1990s, however, Kenyan theater has enjoyed a revival. Small theater groups have been taking plays into the local community and performing in local languages, with Kikuyu groups being particularly successful. Plays such as *Makaririra Kioro*, or *They Will Cry in a Latrine*, which is about a president and his supporters being thrown out of the state house and seeking shelter in a public toilet, proved very popular. The play was written by the late Wahome Mutahi (1954—2003).

A craft store in Nairobi displays figurines of different sizes carved from wood. The tribal figurines are very popular with tourists.

SCULPTURE AND PAINTING

There was little traditional art in East Africa before the arrival of the Europeans, although some groups showed considerable skill in carving and decorating everyday items, such as stools, wooden pillows, or musical instruments. The Kamba were noted for their skillful woodcarving.

The arrival of the Europeans created a new market and many artists turned their attention to carving items such as walking sticks for the British colonists and wooden animal figurines for tourists. Most Kenyan artists concentrated on small items that could be produced quickly and sold for a few shillings; these were dubbed "airport" art and not taken seriously.

In the 1990s a new generation of Kenyan artists emerged. Many were sculptors who built upon the old traditional skills, but young painters such as Michael Soi (1972—) and Shine Tani (1967—) were gaining support. The new generation of artists has borrowed techniques from Europe but retains an African feel in their works. As African art becomes more fashionable, there are better opportunities for Kenyan artists to display their work in Nairobi and in overseas exhibitions.

SOAPSTONE

Soapstone is a soft and smooth stone that can be easily carved, especially when wet. It comes in several colors, the most popular for carving being a dull shade of pink. Most of this stone is found in regions inhabited by the Kisii, who have naturally become the best sculptors.

Sculptors have to cut their own stone from a quarry and then carry it home. They carve it with a knife, polish the carving with sandpaper, and clean it with a brush. The finished product may be left to maintain its natural color or painted with vegetable dyes.

Almost all the sculptures are sold to tourists. Animals, fish, and birds are the favorite subjects. A large statue can take up to three days to produce, while small figurines may be finished in less than an hour. Soapstone may also be used to make plates, trays, small boxes, and candleholders.

The sculptor either sells the pieces to a middleman in the village or more likely takes them to Mombasa or Nairobi and sells them to tourist shops. Several thousand Kisii make their living from carving soapstone and are dependent on Kenya's tourism industry for a living.

MODERN MUSIC

Kenyans love to dance, and a good band can pack a dance hall. Kenyan popular music has been heavily influenced by foreign music. Gospel music, which was brought to Kenya by the early missionaries, remains popular today. In the 1960s and 1970s bands from Tanzania and the Democratic Republic of the Congo came to play in Kenya. Two main styles of Kenyan popular music—*benga* (ben-GAH) and *cavacha* (kah-vah-CHAH)—developed during that period. *Benga* originated on the shores of Lake Victoria and combined modern pop with traditional Luo music. The stars of the period, such as D.O. Misiani (1940—2006) and Daudi Kabaka (1939—2001), are still legends in the Kenyan music world.

Congolese musicians created the fast-paced *cavacha* sound. The lyrics were often sung in the Congolese language of Lingala. Many Congolese musicians who stayed in Kenya later switched to Kiswahili. Tanzanian music also made an impact on the Kenyan scene. Tanzanian songs have a softer sound and are easy to listen to.

In the late 1980s and early 1990s there was less interest in local music, with more Kenyans listening to Western music. Hip-hop and rap revitalized the local music scene. Kenyan rap songs sound similar to rap songs elsewhere but are usually performed in Kiswahili or a tribal language, and the message, often political or social, reflects Kenyan problems.

Joseph Ogidi and Jahd Adonijah began performing and recording their own compositions in 1999. They called themselves Gidi Gidi Maji Maji and had a runaway hit with *Ting Badi Malo*. In 2003 they released *Unbwogable*, a song that became an anthem for opposition politics and reached its peak with the change of government in Kenya.

INTERNET LINKS

www.mbira.org/instrument.html

Website of the Mbira organization, with detailed information on the instrument and links to workshops, lessons, and sound excerpts.

www.africancolours.com/michaelsoi.htm

Online guide to contemporary African art, including works by Michael Soi and Shine Tani.

www.africanreflections.com/cart/

Website with images and descriptions of African art, including Kisii soapstone sculptures.

The National Museums of Kenya (NMK) house specimens and preserved bodies of wildlife as well as archaeological and cultural artifacts. The museums work in partnership with the University of Nairobi and the Institute of African Studies to conduct research on Kenyan cultural history.

LEISURE

A hot air balloon flies low over a herd of wildebeest at the Masai Mara Nature Reserve. Visitors to the reserve can enjoy a panoramic view of wildlife during the ride.

11

N THE PAST, traditional leisure activities in Kenya centered on family and friends. On ceremonial occasions, dancing was the most important form of entertainment. Today, dancing and listening to music are extremely popular, but many Kenyans also enjoy playing sports or watching television. Nairobi and Mombasa offer excellent theaters, cinemas, restaurants, clubs, and cybercafes for the computer literate.

Kenyans go boating on an artificial lake at Uhuru Park, the most popular recreational park in Nairobi.

Many rural Kenyans have migrated to urban centers looking for work and leisure opportunities. Most of the large cities are densely populated. Kenyans living in modern urban cities have mostly shed their tribal customs to adopt a more Western lifestyle. Family and friends remain important and Kenyans enjoy meeting up in coffee shops for a chat. Kenya's favorable climate is ideal for outdoor recreation and sports all year round.

Ajua *also called* bao *is a traditional board game that is one of the most common in Africa. This game is named after the seeds traditionally used as game counters. The seeds are from the wild orange tree* (Toddalia asiatica). *Rules vary from region to region, and the game is quite complicated. Basically, it involves picking up counters— usually seeds, stones, or shells— and distributing them around a board in a way that will capture the opponent's pieces. The board may be an elaborate wood carving with hollows to hold the pieces, or simply some squares scratched in the sand.*

LEISURE TIME IN THE VILLAGE

Kenyans in the countryside love to socialize, tell stories, and play. These activities often seem to be national pastimes. A few simple rural games are part of Kenya's traditional culture. One such game is a version of jacks that is played with stones. This is popular with children, as is checkers. Men are more likely to play *ajua* (a-HOO-ah). Children often amuse themselves without toys, and much of their play consists of simple activities such as running, climbing, and wrestling. Children who live by the sea or lake are likely to spend hours playing in boats, fishing, or swimming. Boys are equally likely to spend their leisure time playing soccer. Often a bundle of rags will be used for a ball, and any tree or even a termite's nest will serve as a goal post.

RURAL LEISURE ACTIVITIES   The land is important to Kenyans. In agricultural areas young boys are encouraged to plant and tend small gardens. Among pastoral groups, young boys spend long hours tending the herds. Often there is little to do, so they may pass their time throwing stones and spears. In the past, when young men were respected for their skills as warriors, these were considered life skills. The time spent herding cattle is also a good opportunity to practice playing musical instruments and to sing traditional songs.

Some leisure activities are specific to certain groups. The Embu people, for example, are skilled stilt walkers, and this forms an important part of their dances during which they wear long black coats and white masks. To acquire this skill, Embu children must spend many hours playing on stilts. While people living along Lake Victoria have canoe races, Kenyans in the most arid areas have a bitter struggle to survive during much of the year. Only after a good rainy season is there any opportunity to relax and enjoy a little leisure time. That is the time for weddings and ceremonies, which will be accompanied by dancing and feasting.

Larger towns offer more organized recreation. Scouting is a popular activity in Kenya. The founder of the Boy Scouts, Baden Powell, is buried in Kenya, and the Scout troop of Nyeri has the honor of keeping his grave weeded and tidy.

Each year, more television sets and radios can be found in the villages. An increasing number of people are using their leisure time to listen to music, stories, and news from around the world.

WORLD'S BEST RUNNERS

Kenya's long-distance runners are among the finest in the world, and the country has produced a long list of Olympic champions. Almost all of Kenya's best athletes come from the Kenyan Highlands. Nobody is sure why that region produces so many world-class athletes. Living at high altitudes is a key element, while many Kenyan athletes claim they became strong runners by having to jog several miles to school each day, so lifestyle appears to be an influence. Diet might be another factor.

In 1964 Wilson Kiprugut became the first black African to win an Olympic track medal when he finished third in the 800-meter race. In 1968 he won a silver medal for the same event. In 1968 Kipchoge Keino won a gold medal in

the 1,500-meter race, and a silver medal in the 5,000-meter race. Naftalia Temu won a bronze medal in the 5,000-meter men's event and gold in the 10,000-meter men's race. The Kenyan Olympic relay team won silver medals in the same year. The star of the team and the man considered to be the father of modern Kenyan athletics was Kip Keino. Kenyan athletes have been winning major titles and breaking records ever since and are particularly strong in cross-country, steeplechase, and marathons.

David Rudisha runs with the Kenyan flag after setting a new world record during the men's 800-m final at the 2012 London Olympics.

KENYA'S TRACK RECORD In 1972 Kenya won a total of nine medals in the Olympic Games, including five gold. Kenya did not go to the 1976 Olympics. The African countries were angry that New Zealand still maintained sporting links with South Africa, and they decided to boycott the Olympics as a protest. It was a great disappointment for the athletes, but many of them continued training and hoped to make up for the missed opportunity in 1980. However, after the former Soviet Union invaded Afghanistan, Kenya again boycotted the Games. This meant that a whole generation of Kenyan athletes never had the chance to prove themselves in the Olympics.

In 1984 Kenya resumed participation in the Olympic Games, and its athletes have done better in each subsequent competition. One medal was won in 1984 for the steeplechase and one for the 10,000-m men's event; seven medals were won in track and field events in 1988; and in 1992 Kenya won eight medals in the track and field events. At that Olympiad two Kenyan runners took the gold and silver medals in the 800-m run, and Kenyans won all three medals in the men's 3,000-m steeplechase. Other medals were won for the 400-m, 5,000-m, and 10,000-m runs. In the 1996 Olympic Games eight medals were won by Kenyan athletes, including a silver medal by Pauline Konga in the 5,000-m women's event. In the 2008 Olympic Games Kenya

In 2011 Samuel Wanjiru fell from the balcony of his home in Kenya and died at the hospital shortly afterward.

KIP KEINO—THE FIRST OF THE GREAT RUNNERS

Kip Keino is the most famous African athlete of all time. He won four Olympic medals—two of them gold—and broke two world records. He will always be remembered for his remarkable versatility and his friendly and modest personality.

Keino was born in a small village in the Nandi Hills close to the Ugandan border. He did not take up running until he was 22, but in his very first year of serious competition, he was selected for the Kenyan team that went to the 1962 Commonwealth Games in Perth, Australia. The year 1966 brought his first major successes and he won two gold medals at the Commonwealth Games in Kingston, Jamaica.

Keino became a national hero and accepted a job in the police force. Like many Kenyans, Keino was a natural athlete, and his European and American rivals were always amazed at how little training he seemed to need.

Keino entered three events at the 1968 Olympics and, despite stomach problems, came away with two medals. In the last event, the 1,500-m race, he scored a spectacular victory over the world record holder and favorite, Jim Ryun. It was a doubly happy day for Keino, for back in Kenya, his wife gave birth to a baby daughter. Four years later, Keino won a second Olympic gold medal, this time in the steeplechase, an event he seldom entered.

Today Keino lives with his wife Phyllis on Kazi Mingi Farm near Eldoret in Western Kenya where they have established the Kip Keino Foundation. This foundation includes a high-altitude training center for athletes, an orphanage, and a school. Helping younger generations is close to Keino's heart as his own parents died when he was very young. In 1987 Sports Illustrated *magazine awarded its Sportsmen and Sportswomen of the Year honor to Keino and seven other "Athletes Who Care" for their humanitarian efforts. In 1996 he was inducted into the World Sports Humanitarian Hall of Fame.*

athletes won a record 14 medals in the track and field events, including five gold medals.

The growing popularity of the marathon has enabled many Kenyans to compete for large prize money. Douglas Wakiihuri is the best-known Kenyan marathon runner, although he did not take up running seriously until he went to Japan as a student. In the 2008 Olympics Samuel Wanjiru won a gold medal in the men's marathon event, and Catherine Ndereba won a silver medal in the women's marathon event. In the 2012 Olympics Ezekiel Kemboi won a gold medal in the men's 3,000-m steeplechase and David Lekuta Rudisha won a gold medal in the men's 800-m event. Silver medals were won in the men's marathon, the women's marathon, the women's 5,000-m event, and the women's 10,000-m event.

The World Cross Country Championships is an annual event. John Ngugi has won the race five times and is regarded as one of the great distance runners in modern sports.

PRESENT-DAY ATHLETES Kenya's star athletes include the 14 medalists from the 2008 Olympics. Three of the five gold medalists were men: Wilfred Bungei in the 800-m, Samuel Wanjiru in the marathon, and Brimin Kipruto in the steeplechase. In the women's events the two gold medalists were Pamela Jelimo in the 800-m and Nancy Lagat in the 1,500-m race. Eleven medals were won by Kenyans in the 2012 Olympics: two gold, four silver, and five bronze medals.

WOMEN ATHLETES For a long time Kenyan women had little impact on track and field. Although they also live at high altitudes, social pressure to marry and have children early made it difficult for women to concentrate on a career in sports. Pioneers such as Susan Sirma (1966 –) and Lydia Cheromei (1977—) led the way, and Kenyan women now regularly feature in major sports events. Joyce Chepchumba (1970—) won a bronze medal in the Sydney Olympics marathon. Marathon runner Lornah Kiplagat set up the High Altitude Training Centre—Iten, Kenya. It is a training camp for athletes from all over the world. The training camp is open to people from recreational level up to Olympic level, for runners, mountain bikers, and sports tourists.

SOCCER

Kenya might be famous in athletics, but soccer is its most popular sport. Soccer has strong ethnic links and can lead to fierce fighting among fans. Traditionally the two big teams are Gor Mahia and AFC Leopards. Gor Mahia represents Nairobi's Luo community, while the Leopards were formed by the city's Luhya community. Although the two clubs have thousands of supporters, they are poorly managed and have not done as well as teams such as Tusker and Sony Sugar, which are sponsored by big companies. The Kenyan national team, Harambee Stars, has had little success and regularly disappoints fans by failing to qualify for the big African and world tournaments.

A group of boys play soccer at a field near their school.

MATHARE UNITED FC The Mathare Valley is a shantytown where more than 900,000 people live in self-made shacks without electricity, clean water, or any other basic facilities. Mathare United was born out of a program that used soccer to give young children in the slums something positive to aim for. In 1998 the team amazed the nation by beating defending champions Eldoret KCC 2-1 in the Moi Golden Cup final. Mathare United joined the Kenyan League in 1999 and won the Moi Golden Cup for a second time in 2000.

The Mathare Youth Sports Association (MYSA) is a self-help body that not only organizes sports activities in Mathare but also encourages young people to contribute to their community by cleaning up the slum. Their aim is to empower young people through sport to help them fulfill their potential and achieve their ambitions and dreams. The MYSA motto is "giving youth a sporting chance on and off the field." In 2012 there were 1,805 soccer teams in 180 leagues across MYSA's 16 zones. Around 14,000 matches are played every year.

Mathare United FC is one of the top teams in Kenya. It was established to give MYSA youth the opportunity to play professional football in their own country. Mathare FC is a separate organization with sponsors. The Mathare United Women FC was formed by MYSA in 2002. In 2006 the team won a gold medal in the East African Tournament, and in the same year won gold in the U16 girls category at the Independence Day Tournament organized by the Ugandan Football Federation.

All the players in Mathare United Women FC and in Mathare United FC come from the MYSA leagues. They are trained to educate peers about HIV/AIDs and perform at least 60 hours of community work each month.

BOXING AND VOLLEYBALL

Kenya has won seven Olympic medals in boxing, including a gold medal in 1988. Overall the sport has suffered from insufficient funds and poor organization. There is a well-supported national boxing league. Competitions are usually won by teams from the army, police force, or prison service.

The Kenyan women's volleyball team was formed in 1987. In that year they won a silver medal in the 4th All-Africa Games in Nairobi. They represented Africa at five FIVB World Championships (1994, 1998, 2002, 2006, 2010), three FIVB World Cups (1991, 1995, 2007), and two Olympic Games (2000, 2004).

OTHER MODERN SPORTS

The annual East African Safari Rally was acknowledged to be one of the toughest car races in the world. The event began in 1953 to celebrate the coronation of Queen Elizabeth II. For many years the Safari Rally started from Nairobi, went around Lake Victoria through Uganda and Tanganyika, and came back to Kenya. In the 1960s the route of the rally was changed to include Kampala and Dar es Salaam. When the border with Tanzania closed in 1969 the rally was no longer allowed to pass through Tanzania. In 1971

Tanzania opened its borders again but insisted that the race begin and finish in Dar es Salaam.

In 2002 the Safari Rally was excluded for the World Championship Rally, but the nostalgia of the original event was recreated by reverting to the characteristics of the East African Safari Rally. Classic cars built before 1974 can enter, but not the powerful and turbo charged 4WD drive cars. The first event was run in 2003 and the second in 2005. Both were won by Kenyans. The most recent running of the East African Safari Classic Rally was in 2009. Now sponsored by the Kenya Commercial Bank (KCB) the rally is now part of the African Rally Championship and is known as the KCB Safari Rally.

Other popular sports include rugby and cricket, which have small but influential followings. The Asian community has also helped to encourage the growth of hockey, cricket, and squash. In 2003 the Kenyan National cricket team surprised everybody by reaching the semifinal of the World Cup. Kenya earned a place as one of the five Associates at the Cricket World Cup 2011 event but was beaten by Zimbabwe.

INTERNET LINKS

www.johnngugifoundation.org/

The official website of the John Ngugi Foundation, a sports organization founded by John Ngugi to help talented young Kenyan athletes to achieve their sporting dreams.

www.kipkeinofoundation.org/

The official website of the Kip Keino Foundation. The primary focus of this foundation is education and the site has links to the many projects with which the foundation is involved.

www.gormahiafc.co.ke/

Official website of the Gor Mahia Football Club with information on the club, team members, and matches.

FESTIVALS

A student wears an elaborate hat during the Kenya Schools and Colleges Drama Festival, where musical troupes come together and compete against other schools in the nation.

12

P UBLIC HOLIDAYS IN KENYA are either religious occasions or anniversaries of important dates in the country's history. Life in Kenya is hard for many people, so they look forward to holidays as an opportunity to celebrate and forget their daily worries. Other people, such as street traders or minibus drivers, cannot afford to take even one day off work and might carry on as usual.

The Indian minority in Kenya celebrate the Hare Krishna Festival. Wax figures and idols are placed on a float as part of a parade.

Kenya's festivals are a mixture of traditional festivals, cultural activities, and sporting events. The most important holiday in Kenya is on December 12, the day on which the country celebrates its independence. There are 10 days designated as public holidays, five of which are religious holidays. These include the Easter holidays of Good Friday and Easter Monday, Christmas Day and Boxing Day, and Eid al Fitr, the end of Ramadhan.

In traditional Kenyan societies, the most important social occasions are those that are age related. Masai boys, at around 16, join the *moran* and remain at this level for between 7 and 14 years. Later this group is promoted to the rank of *ilterekeyani* (il-ter-ek-e-YAHN-ee), or recent elders. From that they pass on to the influential senior elder stage and later to retired elders. The greatest celebration comes at the time of circumcision, which marks a boy's entrance into manhood.

NATIONAL HOLIDAYS

Holidays in Kenya bring out all the excitement and joy of the Kenyan people. In the days leading up to a holiday, overloaded buses take thousands of urbanites back to their villages. Most women try to purchase a new *kanga* (KAN-gah)—a colorful piece of material that wraps around the body like a skirt. There is dancing and probably a village or family feast.

There are four main historical or political celebrations. Madaraka (mah-dar-ah-kah) Day marks the anniversary of self-government on June 1, 1963. This is different from Jamhuri (jam-HOO-roo) Day, December 12, which celebrates the establishment of the new independent nation. Mashujaa Day is observed on October 20, the anniversary of Jomo Kenyatta's arrest in 1952. The three national days are Madaraka Day, Mashujaa Day, and Jamhuri Day, and they are public holidays according to the new constitution of 2010.

CHRISTIAN AND ISLAMIC HOLIDAYS

The most important Christian festivals in Kenya, as in other countries with Christian communities, are Christmas and Easter. At Christmas, people congregate in churches to sing hymns, hear sermons, and socialize. The poor enjoy free dinners served by charitable organizations. People in the cities gather for festive family feasts, and groups travel from house to house, entertaining the residents with carols in Kiswahili.

Public holidays on Good Friday and Easter Monday make for a long Easter weekend for Christians in Kenya to attend church services and celebrate with their families.

THE *KANGA*—A FESTIVAL CLOTH

During any holiday in Kenya, people will meet with friends and show off their best clothes. For many women, a holiday is a reason to buy a new kanga. *The* kanga *is a bright rectangular cotton cloth measuring about 5 feet by 3 feet (1.5 m by 1 m). It can be worn in many different ways. Muslim women often wear them in pairs, called a* doti, *one around the body and one to cover the head and shoulders.*

The first kanga *was made in Mombasa around 1860 by sewing six very large white handkerchiefs together. Designs were hand-printed in black, using a sweet potato or other hard vegetable as a printing block. The cloth is named after the black- and white-spotted African guineafowl, whose name is* kanga *in Kiswahili.*

As the kanga *became popular, traders started to have them specially printed in India and brought to East Africa to trade. The six pieces of cloth were replaced by one piece, and the designs became more colorful and varied.*

Although popular all over East Africa, the kanga *retains a special role in Swahili society. Swahili women may wear a* kanga *known as a* kisutu *(ki-SOO-too) to their wedding. Young girls are presented with their first* kanga *at the beginning of puberty. The* kanga *is worn while praying as part of proper Islamic dress and is placed over a woman's bier at her funeral.*

Boys compete in a donkey race as part of *Maulidi* celebrations. Keeping a donkey moving and on course requires talent, and jockeys spend the entire year honing their skills for the race.

The two major Islamic holidays are Eid al-Fitr and Eid al-Adha. Eid al-Fitr comes after a month of fasting, and Eid al-Adha marks the sacrificing of animals at the end of the pilgrimage. Both are celebrated by Kenya's Muslim population with feasts and prayers in the mosques. In the coastal areas, they are especially important holidays.

The island of Lamu stages a major celebration for *Maulidi*, the birthday of Prophet Muhammad. Such celebrations take place throughout the Islamic world but seldom with the same vigor or energy as on this Kenyan island. The event attracts Muslim visitors from all over East Africa for a week of religious ceremonies and feasting. The side attractions include dancing, donkey races, dhow races, and ritual sword fights.

The lavish celebrations were started in the beginning of the 20th century by Habib Swaleh b. Alawi Jamal al Lail. He was an Arab scholar who studied in Lamu and founded the island's Riyadha Mosque College in 1889.

OTHER SPECIAL OCCASIONS

Although not public holidays, there are several other events on the Kenyan calendar that attract a lot of attention. Some of them are concerned with business and trade. Agriculture is central to the Kenyan economy, and large agricultural shows have always been important occasions. The Agricultural Society of Kenya hosts the Nakuru National Agriculture Show, Mombasa International Show, and Nairobi International Trade Fair in the latter half of the year.

The Kenya International Airshow in Nairobi, although small compared to the European displays, is still one of the most important in Africa. The Ferodo Concours d'Elegance is a competition of old cars and motorcycles that takes place on the Nairobi Racecourse each year. The vehicles are judged on their beauty and condition. Ferodo Concours d'Elegance began in 1970 and has become one of the most significant motoring events in East Africa and a major annual event in Kenya.

There are also events that are linked to the local culture but have been expanded for the tourist industry. These include fishing festivals and the Camel Derby, which is staged in northern Kenya each year. Lamu is famous for its annual donkey race. The race is part of a larger set of cultural celebrations and is held on the waterfront. Donkeys are the main form of transportation on the island, and Lamu residents have become seasoned donkey handlers.

Mombasa's street carnival, first held in 1998, has become a colorful annual event that consists of parades, floats, dancing, music, and the sale of handicrafts. The Ministry of Education organizes a national drama and music festival for primary and secondary schoolchildren. Events take place throughout the country between May and July.

The Rift Valley Festival takes place at Lake Naivasha. This festival celebrates the richness of East African culture and music and showcases a diverse and exciting mix of musical artists and performers from Kenya and abroad. The festival aims to raise funds for the local community in the Lake Naivasha area. Ticket sales profits help to provide a clean, accessible water supply, improved sanitation, and to support projects promoting environmental awareness.

INTERNET LINKS

www.glcom.com/hassan/index.html
This website has a link to information about the *kanga*, including its origins and history.

www.kenyadramafestivals.com/
Kenya National Drama Festival official website.

www.riftvalleyfestival.co.uk/about-us.html
Official website of the Rift Valley Festival.

FOOD

An assortment of colorful fruit at a market in Nairobi, which provide necessary vitamins to supplement the Kenyan diet.

13

KENYA HAS SOME OF the most fertile farmland in Africa and until recently has escaped the famines that have affected other regions of the continent. Staple crops include wheat, potatoes, sweet potatoes, green vegetables, and many types of fruit.

However, many Kenyans are very poor, and their diet is limited by income and the availability of local produce. Many people also have little concept of a healthy diet, and children who eat little apart from carbohydrates often develop pale, reddish hair and suffer from swelling

Kenyans line up at a foodstation in Krisrooa, where they receive beans and maize.

Kenya's food reflects the cultural diversity and the many different lifestyles of the various groups in the country. When the Europeans arrived they brought white potatoes, cucumbers, and tomatoes. The Indians introduced curries and chutneys. Most traditional Kenyan dishes are inexpensive to make and staples are corn, maize, potatoes, and bean.

in the limbs and abdomen. Not surprisingly, Kenya has no great national dishes. The living standard of the majority of people allows for no frills, and food is generally plain.

TYPICAL KENYAN FOOD

Ugali (oo-GAL-ee) forms a major part of the diet for many Kenyans. It is inexpensive and reasonably nutritious, and many poor families depend on it to survive. *Ugali* is usually made from corn ground to form flour and then mixed with water. It is cooked until it forms a thick porridge. Sometimes it is served with vegetables or meat and dipped in gravy. *Ugali* can also be rolled into a hard ball, and people often take these with them when they travel. It is also made from ground cassava or millet.

The Kikuyu grow corn, beans, potatoes, and greens, and their diet is based on these ingredients. One common alternative to *ugali* is *irio* (ay-ree-OH). It is a mixture of fresh potatoes, corn, and peas. Spices and spinach might also be added. *Irio* is a Kikuyu dish. In fact *irio* means food

A young mother and her two daughters grind corn in a wooden mortar and pestle to make *ugali*.

in the Kikuyu language. Similar dishes, known by other names, are cooked in other parts of Africa. Stews form an important part of many diets. They might be eaten with potatoes, rice, *irio*, or *ugali*. The stew might include chicken, goat meat, beef, or just vegetables.

The cattle herders of the arid regions have their own special diet. The Masai, Rendille, Senguju, and Samburu get most of their nourishment from a mixture of milk and cattle blood. The cattle are seldom killed but have their veins punctured. The blood that flows from the wound is collected in a gourd. The Masai only eat meat for special occasions, although they serve it to those who are sick and who need to build up their strength. Fresh meat eaten would usually be goat or sheep as cattle are reserved for sacrifice on ceremonial occasions or major community or family events. Meat is usually roasted over charcoal. The Masai do not eat any wild game or fish, although antelopes are an exception. Many other groups used to hunt for much of their food, and some people still supplement their diet by hunting.

The Turkana people have developed a method of drying milk to preserve it. They also turn some of their herd's milk into ghee (clarified butter) or simply let it go sour. There is a popular recipe that mixes milk with cattle blood and berries to make a cake. The Turkana like to eat meat in stews and soup.

A fresh water vendor in Kenya.

People living in the most arid areas often have to eat whatever is available. The Pokot, for example, hunt virtually every kind of animal, except hyena. Their diet consists primarily of milk, supplemented with a porridge made from wild fruits boiled with a mixture of milk and blood. If the cow is underfed and not producing milk they will drink the blood. The El Molo who live on the southeastern shore of Lake Turkana are competent fishermen and live mainly on fish but also hunt turtles, birds, hippopotamuses, and crocodiles.

The European and Asian communities have largely kept to their own traditional foods. Some items have crossed cultures. The Indian samosa (sah-MOH-sah) is a popular snack food and can be found in most African restaurants. The chapati (chah-PAH-tee), a round Indian flat bread, has also been widely adopted by Kenyan people.

DRINKS

Half of Kenya's population does not have access to clean water, and water scarcity in Kenya has been an issue for decades. The government has provided some good wells, but they can often be a long way from individual houses.

FRUIT SNACKS

Kenyans living in villages supplement their diet by keeping chickens, and most shamba (sham-BAH), or small farms, have fruit trees. Papayas, pineapples, and mangos are some of the most popular fruits. Bananas are a major ingredient in many people's diet. They are not only eaten raw but are also baked, steamed, fried, or roasted. Green bananas, cut into cubes, can be put into stews or soups. Boiled or steamed plantain bananas can also be mashed into a thick mixture called matoke (ma-TOH-kay).

Nandi men and women drink brewed millet beer from a large clay pot.

Many households rely on water collected from the nearest freshwater source, including wells, standpipes, rivers, or lakes.

It is usually the job of women to carry heavy plastic containers of water back to the house. The containers are carried in the traditional manner, on the head or strapped onto the back. If people can afford it, they purchase water from a seller who brings a fresh supply around the village on a cart.

Tea is perhaps the most common drink in Kenya. Poor people drink low-grade tea, and they often add a lot of sugar to sweeten the taste. Coffee is becoming more popular but is usually a social drink to be enjoyed with friends at the end of the day.

Beer is also popular, and East Africa Breweries Ltd is the country's leading branded alcohol beverage business. However, there are many traditional beers that are produced at home. They are called *pombe* (POM-bay) and may be made from corn, bananas, pineapples, or millet. They are often brewed into a drink as thick as oatmeal. On special occasions *pombe* is served from a single large bowl that is passed around a circle of friends.

For ceremonial occasions the Masai have a traditional beer made from honey, an idea borrowed from their Dorobo neighbors. However, today the Masai beer is more likely to be brewed from sugar. Little commercial beer is drunk in the homesteads but Masai men may drink in bars in the townships where they sell their livestock.

Soft drinks are bottled in Kenya and are available in all but the most remote villages. Kenya has even experimented with making an export-quality wine out of papaya.

COOKING KENYAN STYLE

Kenyans have not developed cooking into an art form, but they have created a few interesting recipes that can be considered typical of Kenyan cuisine.

Coconut is often used to make a distinctive and tasty sauce. The coconut is grated and soaked in water in a basket of woven grass. When the basket is squeezed, a coconut-flavored milk oozes out, while the shredded coconut remains trapped in the basket. The coconut milk may be used to cook fish, sometimes with curry, or as a sauce in which to dip *ugali*. Coconut oil is often used for cooking and adds a special rich taste to the food. It also produces a distinctive aroma.

Another popular sauce is made from collard greens or any leafy green vegetable. People call this *sukuma wiki* (soo-KOO-mah WEE-ee), which means finish the week, because it is cheap and used when there is not enough money to buy meat.

Cassava root, also called yuca or manioc, is usually deep-fried and eaten as a snack. It is a major source of carbohydrates.

COOKING UTENSILS

The *mbuzi* is an important tool in Kenyan cooking. It is a small stool with a round, serrated blade fixed at one end. The cook sits astride the *mbuzi* and grates coconut on the blade. Although modern utensils are becoming

A SPECIAL TREAT

In Kenya the most popular edible insect is the termite and they are normally eaten when they begin to fly. At the start of the rainy season, millions of termites leave the ground and fly off in search of new nesting sites. The arrival of the termites causes excitement among some Kenyans, for it means a free, nourishing feast.

The Luo observe termite hills in their area and collect termites when the new ones hatch. Most termites are put into a bag and taken home to be roasted. They are also good as raw, and people chew one or two as they are collecting. Some people remove the wings while others eat them whole. Termites may be served as a delicacy or street snack in some areas, but they are more commonly consumed in the drier areas of Kenya.

A woman cooking by the hearth in her hut.

common, many Kenyans traditionally eat with their hands. The meal is often eaten from one large pot. The men take their food first, followed by the women and finally the children.

As rural homes tend to be very simple, with little furniture, the family is likely to eat outdoors, probably in the shade of a tree. In fact, in some areas it would be considered extremely bad manners to eat indoors during fine weather, as that would prevent any passing friends from joining the meal.

Cooking facilities are basic in the villages, and in many homes food is still cooked over a wood fire. The continual need for firewood has become a serious environmental problem, as trees are being cut down for fuel.

Some people are very superstitious about how food can be prepared. For example, the Nandi live on a basic diet of milk that they believe will be magically contaminated if it comes into contact with metal. Because of this belief, they usually store their milk in a gourd made from a large hollowed-out fruit.

THE FOOD INDUSTRY

Preserving and preparing food is a major industry in Kenya. The coffee and tea industries are an important source of revenue and employ many people. Tea factories are scattered throughout the plantation areas to ease transportation problems. A single factory may need 2,000 to 3,000 pickers to keep it supplied.

More recently, Kenya has diversified its agriculture-linked industries. High-quality fruit is grown and canned on plantations. Great cattle herds support a leather and canned meat industry. Kenya also imports a little cocoa and is one of the few countries in East Africa able to produce high-quality chocolate.

Freshly picked tea leaves go through processing at a factory in Kericho.

INTERNET LINKS

www.daylightcenterpokot.org/index.html

The Daylight Center and School website has a link entitled Nomads in Video that has information on the Pokot diet.

www.maasai-association.org/welcome.html

The official website of the Masai Organization has information on the Masai people, including ceremonies, rituals, and diet.

www.justkenya.org/kenya/recipes/matoke.asp

This website is an online travel guide to Kenya. It has links to information on Kenya culture, festivals, and recipes.

UGALI (CORNMEAL PORRIDGE)

This is a porridge made from cornmeal. Many Kenyans eat it with their meals instead of rice or potatoes. This recipe serves six.

6 cups (1.5 L) water

3 cups (750 ml) cornmeal

Salt and pepper to taste

Put the water into a large saucepan and bring to a boil. Sprinkle the cornmeal into the water and stir for about 25 minutes until it thickens. Add the salt and pepper. Stir continuously as it thickens to prevent burning. If not completely dry, cover and leave to cook on low heat until the *ugali* is quite hard. It can be served as a mashed potato substitute or rolled into small balls. *Ugali* does not have much flavor. It is usually dipped in a stew.

IRIO (VEGETABLE MASHED POTATOES)

Irio is a traditional Kikuyu dish usually consisting of peas, mashed potatoes, and corn. This recipe makes two servings.

1½ cups (375 ml) ripe corn

½ to ¾ cup (125 to 180 ml) shelled peas

Water, for boiling

3 medium potatoes, peeled and cut

2 tablespoons (30 ml) butter

A pinch of pepper

A pinch of salt

Boil the corn and peas in a medium pot filled with water until they become soft. Add the potatoes and boil until they can mash easily. Pour in water whenever necessary. When all the ingredients are soft, mash them with a fork. Add some butter, pepper, and salt.

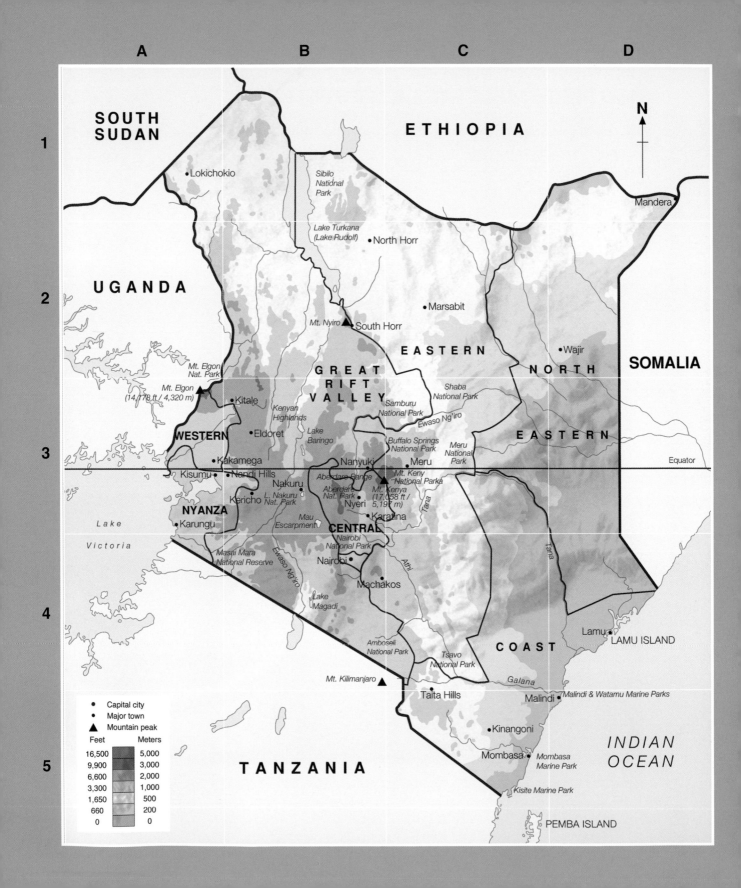

MAP OF KENYA

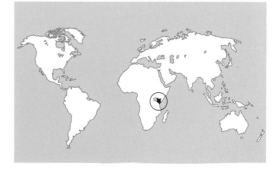

ECONOMIC KENYA

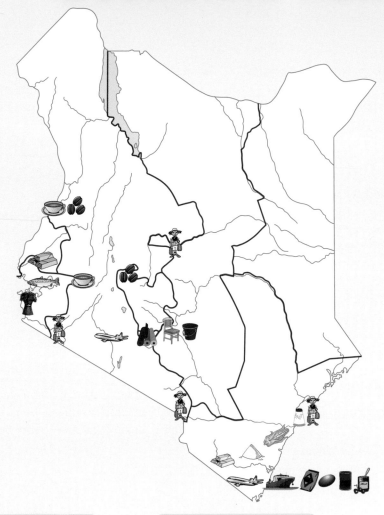

Manufacturing

- Cement
- Furniture
- Gems
- Oil Refinery
- Plastic
- Processed Food
- Textiles

Agriculture

- Coffee
- Corn
- Rice
- Tea

Services

- Airport
- Port
- Tourism

Natural Resources

- Fish
- Gold
- Salt
- Silver
- Soda

ABOUT THE ECONOMY

OVERVIEW

Kenya enjoyed a period of economic growth after it gained independence in 1963. Agriculture, which plays a major role in the country's economy, was badly affected by the El Niño rains and a severe drought in the 1990s. The Kenyan economy is further weakened by corruption. Kenya is reliant on foreign economic aid, which was suspended in 2006 because the government did not succeed in purging corruption from the country's system. Postelection violence and reduced tourism in 2011 caused chronic budget deficits, sharp currency depreciation, and high unemployment. However the Kenyan economy remains hopeful, especially so because of the discovery of commercially viable oil deposits in 2012.

GROSS DOMESTIC PRODUCT (GDP)

$77.14 billion
Per capita: $1,800(2012 estimate)

INFLATION

9.4 percent (2012 estimate)

CURRENCY

1 Kenyan shilling = 100 cents
$1 = 85 KES (October 2013)
Notes: 20, 50, 100, 200, 500, 1,000 shillings
Coins: 5, 10, 20, 50 cents; 1, 5, 10, 20 shillings

GDP SECTORS

Agriculture 26 percent, industry 16 percent, services 58 percent (2012 estimate)

ECONOMIC GROWTH RATE

4.7 percent (2012 estimate)

LABOR FORCE

10.09 million (2012 estimate)

UNEMPLOYMENT RATE

40 percent (2008 estimate)

AGRICULTURE

Coffee, tea, fruit, vegetables, corn, wheat, sugarcane, dairy products, beef, pork, poultry, eggs

INDUSTRIES

Consumer goods (plastic, furniture, batteries, textiles, clothing, soap, cigarettes, flour), agricultural products, horticulture, oil refining; aluminum, steel, lead; cement, commercial ship repair, tourism

MAIN EXPORTS

Tea, horticultural products, coffee, petroleum products, fish, cement

MAIN IMPORTS

Machinery and transportation equipment, petroleum products, motor vehicles, iron and steel, resins and plastics

MAJOR TRADE PARTNERS

China, India, Japan, Tanzania, Uganda, South Africa, Netherlands, United States, United Arab Emirates, United Kingdom

CULTURAL KENYA

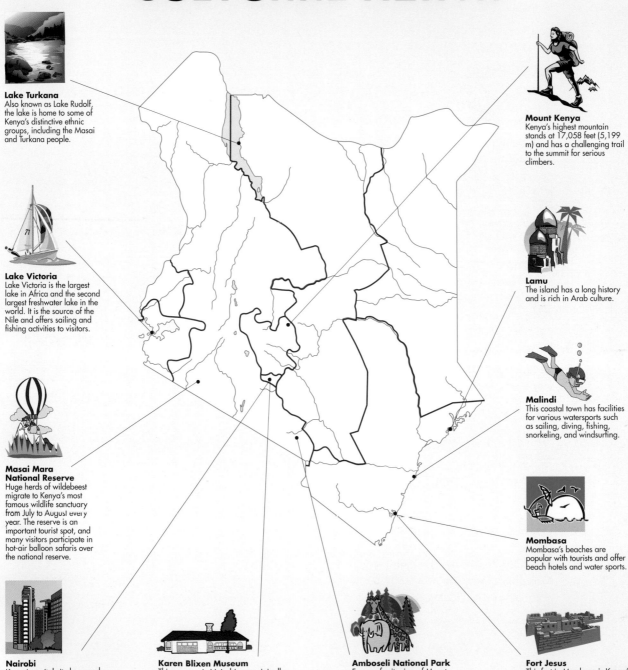

Lake Turkana
Also known as Lake Rudolf, the lake is home to some of Kenya's distinctive ethnic groups, including the Masai and Turkana people.

Lake Victoria
Lake Victoria is the largest lake in Africa and the second largest freshwater lake in the world. It is the source of the Nile and offers sailing and fishing activities to visitors.

Masai Mara National Reserve
Huge herds of wildebeest migrate to Kenya's most famous wildlife sanctuary from July to August every year. The reserve is an important tourist spot, and many visitors participate in hot-air balloon safaris over the national reserve.

Nairobi
Kenya's capital city has good museums, sports, and business facilities and has nurtured a strong dance and music culture.

Karen Blixen Museum
This museum in Nairobi was originally the home of Danish writer Karen Blixen, who lived in East Africa from 1914 to 1931. The 1985 movie Out of Africa was based on Blixen's autobiography.

Amboseli National Park
Famous for its view of Mount Kilimanjaro, this game park is home to a variety of wild animals such as elephants, buffalos, baboons, gazelles, and gerenuks.

Mount Kenya
Kenya's highest mountain stands at 17,058 feet (5,199 m) and has a challenging trail to the summit for serious climbers.

Lamu
The island has a long history and is rich in Arab culture.

Malindi
This coastal town has facilities for various watersports such as sailing, diving, fishing, snorkeling, and windsurfing.

Mombasa
Mombasa's beaches are popular with tourists and offer beach hotels and water sports.

Fort Jesus
This fort in Mombasa is Kenya's most famous historic landmark. Built by the Portuguese in 1593, the fort is now a museum.

ABOUT THE CULTURE

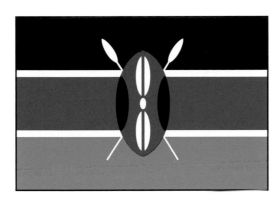

OFFICIAL NAME
Republic of Kenya

CAPITAL
Nairobi

OTHER IMPORTANT CITIES
Mombasa, Kisumu, Nakuru, Machakos, Eldoret, Marsabit, Wajir, Lodwar, Meru

LAND AREA
224,961 square miles (582,646 square km)

ADMINISTRATIVE DIVISIONS
Baringo, Bomet, Bungoma, Busia, Elgeyo/Marakwet, Embu, Garissa, Homa Bay, Isiolo, Kajiado, Kakamega, Kericho, Kiambu, Kilifi, Kirinyaga, Kisii, Kisumu, Kitui, Kwale, Laikipia, Lamu, Machakos, Makueni, Mandera, Marsabit, Meru, Migori, Mombasa, Murang'a, Nairobi City, Nakuru, Nandi, Narok, Nyamira, Nyandarua, Nyeri, Samburu, Siaya, Taita/Taveta, Tana River, Tharaka-Nithi, Trans Nzoia, Turkana, Uasin Gishu, Vihiga, Wajir, West Pokot

POPULATION
44 million (2013 estimate)

POPULATION GROWTH RATE
2.27 percent (2013 estimate)

LIFE EXPECTANCY
63.29 years (2013 estimate)

BIRTH RATE
30.08 births/1,000 population (2013 estimate)

DEATH RATE
7.12 deaths/1,000 population (2013 estimate)

INFANT MORTALITY RATE
42.18 deaths/1,000 live births (2013 estimate)

MAJOR LANGUAGES
English, Kiswahili, numerous indigenous languages

LITERACY RATE
87.4 percent of adults more than 15 years old can read and write (2010 estimate)

ETHNIC GROUPS
Kikuyu 22 percent, Luhya 14 percent, Luo 13 percent, Kalenjin 12 percent, Kamba 11 percent, Kisii 6 percent, Meru 6 percent, other African 15 percent; non-African (Asian, European, Arab) 1 percent

MAJOR RELIGIONS
Protestants, Roman Catholics, Muslims, Traditionalists

TIMELINE

IN KENYA	IN THE WORLD
500 B.C. Bantu people migrate to East Africa.	**116–117 B.C.** The Roman Empire reaches its greatest extent, under Emperor Trajan (98–17).
A.D. 700 Arabs settle along the coast and introduce Islam to Kenya.	**1000** The Chinese perfect gunpowder and begin to use it in warfare.
15th century Nilotic tribes migrate south from Sudan.	
1498 Vasco de Gama arrives in Kenya.	**1530** Beginning of trans-Atlantic slave trade organized by the Portuguese in Africa.
1720 End of the Portuguese empire in East Africa	**1789–99** The French Revolution
1846 Christian missionaries arrive from Europe.	**1869** The Suez Canal is opened.
1884 Berlin Conference divides Africa into spheres of influence.	
1890 Kenya is declared a British protectorate.	
1893 Coffee is introduced to Kenya.	**1914** World War I begins.
1920 Kenya is declared a British colony.	**1939** World War II begins.
1944 Kenyan African Union (KNU) formed to campaign for African independence.	**1945** The United States drops atomic bombs on Hiroshima and Nagasaki.
1947 Jomo Kenyatta becomes leader of the KAU.	**1949** The North Atlantic Treaty Organization (NATO) is formed.
1952 to 1956 State of emergency is declared in response to Mau Mau rebellion against the British.	**1957** The Russians launch Sputnik.
1963 Kenya gains independence. Jomo Kenyatta is prime minister.	
1964 Kenya becomes a republic. Jomo Kenyatta becomes president and Odinga vice-president. Wilson Kiprugut wins first Olympic medal for Kenya.	
1966 Odinga leaves Kanu after ideological splita and forms rival Kenya People's Union (KPU).	**1966–1969** The Chinese Cultural Revolution
1969 Government minister Tom Mboya is killed. KPU is banned and Odinga is arrested.	
1974 Jomo Kenyatta is reelected as president.	

IN KENYA	IN THE WORLD
1977 Hunting of wild animals banned in Kenya **1978** Kenyatta dies; Daniel arap Moi succeeds as president. **1982** Kenya is officially declared a one-party state by the National Assembly. **1991** Special conference of KANU agrees to introduce a multiparty political system. **1992** Moi reelected in multiparty elections. KANU wins majority. **1994** Odinga dies. Opposition groups form a coalition, the United National Democratic Alliance. **1997** Demonstrations call for reform; Moi wins further term in widely criticized elections. **2002** KANU voted out of power. Kibaki becomes president. **2003** International Monetary Fund (IMF) resumes lending to Kenya after a 3-year gap, citing anticorruption measures. **2004** Food crisis caused by crop failure and drought. **2005** Parliament approves a draft constitution which is rejected by voters; President Kibaki replaces his cabinet. **2007** Government and opposition agree to share power and a cabinet is signed in April. **2010** New constitution approved in referendum. It is designed to limit the powers of the president and devolve power to the regions. **2012** ICC rules that several politicians must stand trial over the 2007 postelection violence. **2013** Elections are held; Uhuru Kenyatta of The National Alliance Party becomes president.	**1986** Nuclear power disaster at Chernobyl in Ukraine 1991 Break-up of the Soviet Union **1997** Hong Kong is returned to China. **2001** Terrorists crash planes in New York, Washington, D.C., and Pennsylvania. **2003** War in Iraq

GLOSSARY

Bajuni (ba-JOON-i)
A Bantu group of Kenya.

Bantu (BAHN-too)
An ethnic or linguistic group in Africa, such as the Ndebele and Shona.

baobab
An African tree with a thick trunk that stores water.

bwana (BWAH-nah)
Short for *baba wa wana*, meaning the father of many sons, a traditional way to address men.

Cushitic
A family of African languages.

harambee (hah-rahm-BAY)
A Kiswahili word that means pull together.

jambo (JAM-boh)
Kiswahili for hello.

kanga (KAN-gah)
A colorful cloth wrapped around the body.

kari-bu (kar-i-BOO)
Kiswahili for welcome.

Kikuyu
A group of African people originally from the area of Mount Kenya.

laibon (LAI-bon)
A Masai fortune-teller.

Masai
A Nilote tribe of cattle raisers of Northern Kenya.

matoke (ma-TOH-kay)
A dish made from cooked bananas.

mbira (m-BIR-ah)
A thumb piano with a wooden soundboard and metal strips of varying lengths that are plucked to produce a melody.

mbuzi (m-BOO-zee)
A tool used for grating coconut.

moran (MAH-ren)
The warrior rank of the Masai.

ngoma (n-GO-mah)
A large drum played in traditional Kenyan music that is made of a hollowed-out section of a tree trunk and an animal skin stretched over the top.

Nilotic
A group of languages from the area of the Nile.

obukano (o-boo-KAHN-o)
A stringed musical instrument.

pombe (POM-bay)
A traditional Kenyan beer made from corn, bananas, pineapple, or millet.

ugali (oo-GAL-ee)
The staple food of East Africa made from corn, millet, or cassava flour.

FOR FURTHER INFORMATION

BOOKS

Dinesen, Isak. *Out of Africa.* New York: Random House, 2002.

Estes, Richard D., Otte, Daniel (illustrator), and Fuller, Kathryn S. *The Safari Companion: A Guide to Watching African Mammals.* Vermont: Chelsea Green Publishing Company, 1999.

Ham, Anthony, Butler, Stuart and Starnes, Dean. *Lonely Planet Kenya (Country Guide).* Melbourne: Lonely Planet, 2012.

Leakey, Richard and Morell, Virginia. *Wildlife Wars: My Fight to Save Africa's National Treasures.* New York: St. Martin's Press, 2001.

Lemasolai-Lekuton, Joseph and Viola, Herman. *Facing the Lion: Growing Up Maasai on the African Savanna.* Washington, DC: National Geographic Children's Books, 2005.

Maathai, Wangari. *The Green Belt Movement: Sharing the Approach and the Experience.* New York: Lantern Books, 2003.

Nabwire, Constance and Montgomery, Bertha. *Cooking the East African Way.* Minneapolis, MN: Lerner Publications Company, 2001.

Western, David. *In the Dust of Kilimanjaro.* Washington, DC: Shearwater Books, 2001.

MUSIC

Rough Guide to Music of Kenya and Tanzania. Various artists. World Music Network, 1996.

The Nairobi Beat: Kenyan Pop Music Today. Various artists. Rounder Select, 1992.

Kenya Dance Mania. Various Artists. Earthworks, 2009

DVDS

Out of Africa. Universal Studios, 2000.

The Flame Trees of Thika. A&E Home Video, 2005

Our Planet: The Kenya Story. Razor Digital Entertainment, 2001

BIBLIOGRAPHY

BOOKS

Adamson, Joy. *Born Free: A Lioness of Two Worlds.* New York: Pantheon, 1960.

Azevedo, Mario (editor). *Kenya: The Land, the People, and the Nation.* North Carolina: Carolina Academic Press, 1993.

Burch, Joann J. *Kenya: Africa's Tamed Wilderness.* New York: Maxwell Macmillan International, 1992.

Houston, Dick. *Safari Adventure.* New York: Dutton Juvenile, 1991.

Ng'Weno, Fleur. *Focus on Kenya.* Vermont: Trafalgar Square, 1992.

WEBSITES

Central Intelligence Agency World Factbook (select Kenya from the country list). www.cia.gov/cia/publications/factbook

East African Cross Borders Biodiversity Project.x-borderbiodiversity.tripod.com/

Friends of Lake Victoria conservation group. www.osienala.org

General information and news. www.kenyaweb.com

Kenya Radio Stations Live. www.surfmusic.de/kenia.htm

iWay Africa. www.iwayafrica.com/

East African Standard. www.eastandard.net

Lewa Wildlife Conservancy. www.lewa.org

INDEX

INDEX